KEEP THE BANNER WAVIN'

by

Daniel E. Johnson IV

WOLF CREEK PRODUCTIONS
Beyond Wolf Mountain Series

i

Beyond Wolf Mountain Series

Published by
WOLF CREEK PRODUCTIONS
c/o John M. Cook, Jr.
PO Drawer L
Norris, SC 29667
http://j-cook.home.mindspring.com

Printed by
MORRIS PUBLISHERS
3212 E. Hwy 30
Kearney, NE 68847
800-650-7888
http://morrispublishing.com

Printed in the United States of America

First Edition

10 9 8 7 6 5 4 3 2 1

Library of Congress Cataloging-in-Publication Data

Johnson, Daniel E., IV

Keep the Banner Wavin' : Story of a North Carolina Mountain Preacher / Daniel E. Johnson, IV
1. United States--History--Genealogy--Cook.
2. Genealogy--History--Cook 3. Mountain life--history
ISBN 0-9714630-0-X
Library of Congress Control Number 2001118987

INTRODUCTION

This book has been one that I have long carried in my heart, with it's title ringing in my ears since I heard the phrase referred to often times in countless visits with my older family members growing up in Washington state. Grandpa Floyd Cook has since become my hero and one whose life I would like to personally emulate.

Mountain people, especially the Tarheels of North Carolina, are special—very special in my book. To some outsiders, on the negative side they have the reputation for being rough, ill mannered and stubborn; but for those who take the time to learn and listen, they are tenderhearted, giving, generous, sincere and altogether deeply loving. They love to laugh!! It is my hope that some of this endearing quality comes through. I am proud to be a Tarheel...(even a 'displaced' one!)

In 1988 I had the tremendous joy of preaching in Balsam Grove Baptist Church, a small country church that was pastored by Grandpa Floyd for several years. That same day, a dear old man, Rev. Sterling Milton (pillar in the Caney Fork community) was there. When he discovered who I was, after the sermon he commented to a cousin, 'That young man up there preaches, and acts and LAUGHS just like his great great grandfather!' Sterling had known Grandpa Floyd as a young man, remembered him all those years, and served to bridge a 70 year gap to convey a continuity from ancestor to descendant.

This has been a labor of love that I have thoroughly enjoyed, and one that has served to strengthen the ties of the Cook clan, both on the East and West Coast. The legacy of Grandpa Floyd is one that must be preserved, especially in the shifting sand of eroding cultural values that we see all around us. Proverbs 10:7 says, *"The memory of the just is blessed..."* and it is my hope that our collective memory of Grandpa Floyd Cook will be sustained for many years to come, for our children, and our children's children.

I have loved getting acquainted with 'kin' through this project, and thank the Lord for the new relationships and bonds that have been formed. It is with a great sense of satisfaction that I present this book to all of my family, as a gift and a token of my love for you all.

Until the next one!

Danny

DEDICATION

To my Grandma Winnie Cook Pyatte LeKey
*(already gone home to be with
Jesus—there'll never be another one like her!!)*

and her sisters, Naomi, Minnie, and Clara
*(also found around the throne of God,
they'll all be a SHOUTIN' for sure!)*

**and our remaining matriarch of the family
Dolores (Dee)**

**Each one of them with their
unique personality,
sense of humor and
home-spun character have
transmitted to all of us
the values of what it means
to be part of the Cook clan,
and have contributed greatly
to whom I personally am today.**

I love you.

With the exception of the following fictional composite characters, all characters mentioned are real persons:

Alf
Dock
The Jones boys
Grampa Grant
Old man Hindershal
The Ledbetters
Ana Lar Parker
Rev. Furthermore Quint
Sassafras Walker

FOREWORD

The **Beyond Wolf Mountain** project began several years ago as we would go to family reunions and gatherings and hear stories of our ancestors who had lived before us. I had always enjoyed hearing about the life they lived in the mountains of North Carolina and the stories of my Great-great-grandfather Solomon Floyd Cook who had served in the Civil War and died in a POW camp in Chicago. But mostly all I did was listen. For years, on our branch of the family, we have relied on our self-proclaimed family historian Uncle Leland to provide us with the oral stories. I realized that someone would have to carry on the tradition or the next generation would lose the stories that show where our family has come from and hopefully will help guide us to where we need to go.

Wanting to find out more about our family, I started visiting relatives, going to libraries and searching the internet where I found several pieces of our family history and was able to make contact with other descendants of Hence (Henson) Marvin Cook who were researching their branch of the family. I ran across Dan Johnson, a missionary in Central America, and we started emailing back and forth. Soon I realized Dan had a wealth of information on Henson's son Ethan Allen Cook and challenged him to put it down on paper to share with the rest of the family. Boy was I surprised when about a month later he contacted me said that he had the first draft of *Keep the Banner Wavin'* ready which was about his great great grand father William Floyd

Cook who was a mountain preacher in North Carolina who inspired four generations to follow into the ministry.

Hopefully this will be the first of many books that we will put together about our family in the **Beyond Wolf Mountain** project. Other subjects we plan to explore are Solomon Floyd Cook who fought in the Civil War and died as a POW, the midwife who helped birth several thousand children, or the ones who worked in the timber industry who had to move west when the blight killed off the Chestnut trees of North Carolina. If anyone has a suggestion for a book or would like to write one and have it included in the series, please contact us at j-cook@mindspring.com or at the address on the copy write page.

For years, most of what I knew of my family history on my father's side went back to Wolf Mountain in Jackson County, NC where my grandfather grew up. The third Sunday of every August most of my uncles, aunts and cousins would come to town and we would load up and drive 2 hours along the winding dirt and gravel mountain roads to reach the cemetery where my great grand parents Marion Monroe Cook and Ann Bone are buried for the annual grave decoration service. We would help clean the graves and put flowers on them and then a local preacher would bring a message. After a picnic we would ride up to the site of the family home place and visit with a couple of families that my grandpa grew up with. Then we would make the journey back home. We would repeat this trip almost every year.

I knew there had to be more information about the family history. The idea behind the name for the **Beyond Wolf Mountain** project was to find out where the family had come from and where they went after many moved from the mountains. Also the thought was to explore the influence our family has had on their community and the world **Beyond Wolf Mountain**. In other words, I wanted to expand my knowledge of our family history **Beyond Wolf Mountain.**

Usually it is difficult to know exactly what was said in conversation and done in action for people who lived in the past, say 100 years ago. By looking at genealogical and historical records along with family tales, traditions, personal letters and diaries we have been able to piece together a reasonably accurate portrayal of the subject. Only if we could go back in time and actually visit our ancestors, to live with them and ask them questions, could we have a more accurate view of their lives. Instead of just presenting facts, we have tried to build a story around the life of our lead character. Robert Morgan authored the award winning **Gap Creek,** which is a story about the first years in the marriage of his grandmother who lived in North and South Carolina. Robert advises anyone writing a historical based book that we should tell the story so that it is real and you feel you are actually there and not just recite historical facts by creating "a sense of real characters and a real story by putting down one vivid detail, one exact phrase, at a time."

Hopefully we have done this.

John M. Cook, Jr.

ACKNOWLEDGMENTS

Every author knows that his or her work is highly dependent on others and this one is no exception. First of all, I want to thank my Lord and Saviour Jesus Christ, for the life He has given me, and the constant stream of fulfilled dreams that He delights in giving me, one of the latest being the publication of this book. Hallelujah!!

Next I would like to thank my cousin and friend, John Cook Jr., who has served as the primary 'push' and encouragement in this project, his love for history, accuracy, details, scholarship and excellence have motivated me greatly, not to mention his proof-reading, corrections, suggestions and 'footwork' to get this printed!! I also want to say a big thank you to his wife Denise, for patiently 'lending' her husband for hours on-end to this fascination of ours!! May the Lord bless you!

To name all of the family members whose memories and 'visits to the attic' have served me so greatly are too many to name; but there are a few who have put in extra hours and tolerated my incessant "hey I have one more question": Anna Awald, Donna Booker, J.B. Cook, Carroll Ensley, Naomi Hooper Green, Doris Groves, Ruby Huston, Alice Sitton, Judy Sutton and Marie Watson.

For research consultation and a willing hand, Ruth Shular of the Jackson County Genealogical Society, thank you so much.

For those who have helped in the preparation and publishing: Martha Smith Evatt (retired librarian) who spent many hours in fine tuning our proof-reading; Andy and John Cook, for their wonderful hand in the cover design, God's blessings on you!

As with all genealogical works, this is an on-going project of revision and correction. Trying to track down some 700 descendants, their spouses, and children and verify all relevant information is a gigantic task. The author assumes full responsibility for errors and solicits any corrections, additions, etc. to be sent to him: djohnson@c.net.gt In any future publications, those changes will happily be made.

"THIS CHILD IS SET FOR THE FALL AND RISING AGAIN OF MANY..."

Chapter 1

"They God, hits another boy! Praise you Jesus!" proclaimed the midwife as William Floyd Cook entered the world on August 16, 1865. His birth paralleled another 'birth' that was taking place in the United States, the slow, painful birth of a 'new' nation after the long and bloody Civil War. 'Floyd' as he would be known throughout his entire life, had been conceived during a quick time of unexpected furlough when his farmer father, who grudgingly had signed up with the Confederate forces, was home on leave in November of 1864. The war had been long and hard, and was grinding down to its inevitable end. Morale was low in the south, especially in the Appalachians. The economy had never been strong in this part of the country, and while it had offered great promise since the golden period of settlement and exploration of the 18th century, it was always a hard life to be found there. The war just added insult to injury and made a difficult life, that much more of a struggle.

Floyd was often in the shadow of his older brothers, and at times it didn't seem that anything special would come of his life—he was kind of lost in the middle, as so often happens in large families. But his mother, to whom many would come for counsel and a sound word of advice (if not a verbal thrashing, often, looked askance at her fourth son, wondering what it was that was different about him. Even in his childhood, slowly but surely the depth of Floyd's character began to unfold.

All of the kids loved to hear talk about the war. But it wasn't always easy to get their uncles or fathers to talk about it. First of all, there was some division of opinion when it came to war and politics, and it normally ran along generational lines. Floyd's grandpa, Henson Marvin Cook, prior to the war had been a staunch Democrat—but once North Carolina separated from the Union, he opposed the war and voted Republican for the rest of his life. In his application for amnesty he wrote:

> *"I was not and never have been a Postmaster under the United States Government. The office aforesaid having been created during the rebellion, I took it as an accommodation to my neighbors and friends. This I suppose is my only offense to the government of the United States. I was always and still am a Constitutional Union Man, and opposed the act of secession, and before the act of secession always*

acted with the Democratic Party, But after my state, the state of North Carolina by a convention of the people went out of the federal union. I then felt it was my duty to abide by their decision. I have not been with the army of the state of North Carolina, or that of the Confederate States, but as a citizen of North Carolina performed all the requirements of my state during the rebellion."

(Application for Amnesty dated 29 May 1865)

But in spite of Hence's unwavering support of the Union, his sons felt otherwise, and all six of them served in the Confederate Army, two of them giving their lives. So conversations about the war were often dictated by those present, and a respect for the variety of opinion that existed.

Floyd had at least eight uncles who were all Confederate soldiers along with his father. *[Solomon Floyd Cook, Henry Benson Cook, Samuel Riley Cook, James P. Cook, William J. Cook, Daniel Hamilton Wood, Henry Houston Wood, James Madison 'King' Wood]* Two of them died, one (William J. Cook) during the conflict, and the other (Solomon Floyd Cook) in a Union POW camp in Illinois— from these two heroic uncles, our William Floyd derived his name. Uncle Sam Riley and Uncle Jim had deserted early on in their military service, and while no one held them to blame (there were many others who did the same) neither one of them seemed to ever get over a sense of shame. This was especially true knowing that two of their own brothers had given their life's blood—but no one seemed to know what for? Floyd's daddy Ethan, or his Uncle Henry, were much more apt to talk about the war, if they were prodded and in the right mood. Uncle Henry had converted to Christ shortly after the war, and became a preacher of the gospel; he was an excellent communicator and often held his audience spellbound. The subject of the war however was still painful, and he was reluctant to talk about the things he saw and experienced. But to find a honest-to-goodness, dyed-in-the-wool, Confederate-to-the-core military man in the mountains, was no small chore. However, once in a while one would come around to visit and 'pay respects', and was inevitably obliged to tell, to the delight of many listening ears, of a past glory that was once the confederacy. One such man was 'Cotton' Tom Hooper, first cousin to Floyd's momma—why he'd even been a prisoner of war in a Yankee prison!!

"Wale, it's like this younguns,'...and off he would go, telling the tales of a generation past, that almost everyone in the valley hoped would never be repeated.

'Cotton' Tom Hooper was a family man when the war started. He'd been married six years and had three children and another one on the way when the cannons fired at Ft. Sumter. Everyone had hoped it would soon be over, and especially the folks in the mountains felt that it was far away from them, and far away from their reality. In the first place, almost no one had slaves in their part of the country—it wasn't for a philanthropic interest or a firm conviction in that 'all men are created equal,' it was simply the fact that no one had money to buy and keep up slaves. Well...there was more to it than that actually. The question of slavery and slaveholding was never simple in the south, especially during the Great War. But one other factor that influenced these rugged Scotch-Irish descendents was their doggoned independent (some would say stubborn) streak. They wouldn't have someone else do for them what they could do for themselves. Black, white, red, no matter. They were proud to eke out a living with their own two hands, and the sweat of their brow.

And Cotton Tom was no different—he was a mountain man, and just like the rest of his friends and neighbors, never believed this war would get as far, or last as long, as it did.

When the state of North Carolina put out its call for volunteers, there was no lack in manpower. While the mountaineers had little interest in fighting the 'high falutin' lowlander's battle (as they saw it), they were as 'Tarheel' as you could get. 'Tarheel' was a term that had risen during the Revolutionary War, from the exemplary fighting of North Carolina's troops in the Continental Army. They were often the last ones to leave the battlefield, and quickly became known as 'tarheels'—their feet just stuck to the earth without surrendering. So it was as much a matter of pride and defending ones own turf from invasion, that many of North Carolina's sons rushed to sign up.

When the "cruters" (recruiters) came to Jackson County in July of 1862, there were long lines at the makeshift recruiting office that had been set up at Webster, the county seat. This was not the first time they'd been through, but things were getting worse.

Just a couple of months earlier, the battle of Shiloh had been fought in Tennessee, a bloody battle and much too close to home for comfort. The mood of the country was changing, and there was tension in the air. Out of that gruesome exchange, a poem was penned and put to music by Will Shakespeare Hays, and he rapidly gripped the whole country, both north and south, as both had paid already a high price. This poem did a great deal to stir the passions of its citizens:

> *On Shiloh's dark and bloody ground,*
> *   the dead and wounded lay,*
> *Amongst them was a drummer boy,*
> *   that beat the drum that day;*
> *A wounded soldier raised him up,*
> *   his drum was at his side,*
> *He clasped his hands and raised his eyes,*
> *   and prayed before he died;*
>
> *Look down upon the battle field,*
> *   Oh Thou our Heavenly friend,*
> *Have mercy on our sinful souls,*
> *   the soldiers cried, 'AMEN!'*
> *For gathered round a little group,*
> *   each brave man knelt and cried,*
> *They listened to the drummer boy,*
> *   who prayed before he died:*
> *'Oh Mother!' said the dying boy,*
> *   'Look down from heaven on me,*
> *Receive me to thy fond embrace,*

oh take me home to thee.
I've loved my country as my God,
*   to serve them both I've tried,'*
He smiled, shook hands, death seized
*   the boy who prayed before he died.*

Each soldier wept then like a child,
*   stout hearts were they and brave,*
The flag his winding sheet,
*   God's book the key unto his grave;*
They wrote upon a simple board,
*   these words, 'This is a guide'*
To those who mourn the drummer boy,
*   who prayed before he died."*

["The Drummer Boy of Shiloh, p. 76, The Confederate Reader, The Civil War Reader, ed. By Richard B. Harwell, Mallard Press, BDD Promotional Book Co. Inc., 666 Fifth Ave., NY, NY 10103. ISBN: 0-7924-5601-7]

A poem, a song, rallied both sides of the deeply divided nation, and the mountain folk were just as passionate. On the day of inscription, Cotton Tom was one of the first ones there—the Confederate Army was offering several different types of service, with varying times, but Cotton Tom went for it all. He signed up for '3 years or the war.' He was now officially part of Company G, of the 62nd Regiment of the North Carolina Infantry, C.S.A.! Boy was he proud! His wife Mary was too, she had to admit—but once he got that uniform on, she had to brush away her tears for the fear that gripped her about their future. Here she was with three younguns, and another one on the way, and her husband is galavantin' off to war!

Company G was made up of Jackson county boys, if they weren't all closely related, they certainly did know each other. In fact, Floyd's pa, and his Uncles Sol and Henry were all part of the same regiment. 'We's all kindy 'sited,' said Cotton Tom as he went on with his story.

At one point, Cotton Tom was shot:

> *"(he) was shot 'through and through' with a mini-ball. He lay in the swamp for 4 days without food or water. He then crawled back out and made his way across a field about ½ mile to a small shack owned by a black woman. She nursed him back to health and he then re-entered the army..."*

[Quote from Naomi Hooper Green in *"A Glimpse into the Past' of Hooper and Related Families (1763-1998)* by Mary Hooper Crocker, p. 584. Used by permission]

The second time in the army, their regiment hadn't seen a lot of action—in fact, there were a few lull times, where they were even permitted a quick furlough home, especially because they were so close anyway. In September of 1863 several Confederate regiments had united, part of Company G of the 62nd NC Infantry included. They were in Cumberland Gap, Tennessee and though they were 2,500 strong, the Union Army was larger. Twice surrender was demanded, and both times refused. Finally, a third time it was demanded once again, and this time, the demoralized Confederates were obliged to surrender. *[The Union Army, vol. 5, p. 333 A History of Military Affairs in the Loyal States 1861-65—Records of the Regiments in the Union Army—Cyclopedia of Battles—Memoirs of Commanders and Soldiers, Madison: Fed. Publ. (1908)]* As quick and easy as that, these proud, hard-working responsible mountain men were led like docile lambs to their fate. They were sent to a POW camp in Illinois*; [ibid]* the conditions were awful. Of course the food was barely palatable, medical care was lacking, and cleanliness was a thing of the past. Plus, the weather was changing, and few of these southerners had ever seen a Chicago area winter. They were sick, some of them wounded, and all of them longing to be with their families and restart their lives. But for some of them, it was never to be. They survived the battles, only to die of sickness.

Fall turned into winter...and then spring, and summer. And the cycle started all over again. After a year in this 'hell hole' Cotton Tom had seen several of his companions 'pass on to the other side' among them Floyd's Uncle Sol. News was scarce and rumors were abundant—the boredom was enough to drive any man mad, but it was made worse by the daily rumor mill, sometimes promising freedom by the end of the week, other times threatening firing squads by direct order of the commanding officer of the Union forces, General Grant. They did have the solace and freedom of writing letters, *[e.g. Letters of Solomon Floyd Cook]* as they were able to scrape together paper and pencil to do so, and for some this was a ritual that kept their hope alive. Those who didn't know how to read and write, had to channel their energies in some other way.

It was finally in June of 1865, almost two years later, that the nightmare of these brave survivors came to an end. Though General Robert E. Lee surrendered to Grant in April, it was just a week later, that the country was in turmoil following the brutal assasination of President Lincoln. This turned into a bureaucratic nightmare concerning the release of prisioners of war, and it wasn't until later in the summer that they were finally 'processed' and sent home. After they were forced to recite and sign the 'oath of allegiance' they were finally set free, and made the long trek to their waiting families.

It was these kinds of stories that molded and formed Floyd's early thought and convictions. There wasn't a family gathering that went by, where some allusion wasn't made to the Great War. It had been the biggest thing that had happened in the mountains ever, and especially the young folks Floyd's age never tired of asking about what happened, who was there, what did you do and all kinds of smiliar typical interrogations. Floyd decided early on in life that he didn't like war a'tall and he never wanted to be a part of something so terrible.

"...A SPIRIT PASSED BEFORE MY FACE, THE HAIR OF MY FLESH STOOD UP..."

Chapter 2

Judaculla Rock. Simply the reference to this interesting bit of geography was sure to elicit a reponse. Among the very young, it was the subject of countless fears, and ill-told nighttime stores by older siblings; among the teenagers, it was a place to be avoided, and always cloaked in mystery; and among the adults, the subject of stories and speculations they had heard from their grandparents, that left them in a state of questioning.

The rock itself is actually quite non-descript—a somewhat large rock, more than haflway imbedded in the ground, located between a couple of farms off of the beaten track of Caney Fork Road. What causes such speculation, are the curious pockmark- like markings that cover it, as well as some undecipherable Indian-like hieroglyphics. It has been in this same location for longer than even the oldest can remember, and no one has any idea as to the meaning of these curious symbols.

Of course, all of this adds up to something to kill the time, especially to pre-adolescent boys with nothing to do after all their chores are taken care of. It was precisely this scenario into which Floyd walked as an unwitting accomplice one day.

They never lacked for companions and friends, fishing partners and just someone to idle around with in this part of the country. Every family was related in some way or another, and most of them by far had at least six or seven children. When there was nothing to do, and nothing to keep them entertained, these young creative imaginations would soar, inventing things to do to pass the time.

It turns out that Floyd and several of his friends and cousins were down at their favorite fishin' hole, when they got to talking about Judaculla Rock. Each one of them had his own knowledge to add to the subject, and as the afternoon wore on, the stories became more agitated and exaggerated. Floyd had never liked to go very near to the rock alone, figgerin' it better to be safe then sorry. He wasn't real superstitious, like so many of the other kids— but at any rate, he didn't like to fool with things that he didn't understand either.

'Hey Floyd, you ain't said nothin' yet, what ch'all think?' cried out Alf from the other side of the creek. 'No, I don't know hardly nothing 'bout that there ol' rock—my granpappy told me once that there'd been some Indians that lived right close there.' 'Wall, I'll tell you one thing, I think you're chicken, that's done fer sure; yous not said much 'cause you're 'fraid to go by it.' 'Not true,' Floyd quickly replied. Dock quickly chimed in, 'Alf's right...Floyd's ascared to go by that ol' rock, 'specially at night!' This whole adolescent conversation quickly turned into a struggle for manhood, with jokes and jabs, and finally a dare. 'Floyd Cook, I dares you to go to Judaculla Rock tonight—and if yer man enough, bring us back this ol' lead rope that I'll go and leave right tway. You bring it back to us all tomorry an' we'll know fer sure that yer no skirdy cat.'

Floyd was just coming into his adolescent years, and there was always some kind of unspoken coming-of-age type of trial, that sooner or later every boy in the valley was subject to. He'd already started smoking, a habit that all the boys got into early on; their parents slightly scolded them, but with no conviction as to its real harmfulness. Anyway, most of these boys' fathers smoked, and several of their mothers chewed 't'backy,' so it was a natural development and habit that formed, that was often accompanied by a perceived and oft-repeated benefit to one's health! After all, "Grampa smoked for 30 years and never had a sick day in his life!" This habit which had rooted itself in Floyd's tastes, would stay with him all his life, and have a serious consequence to it, and right when he least could afford it. So this was one test he'd already passed...but Judaculla Rock?? He couldn't refuse, not with all his friends and cousins looking on him right now, wondering what his answer would be. 'Yeah I'll go—I'll shows ye that Floyd Cook's no sissy.' The rest of the boys jabbed each other and giggled, proud of their hastily arranged dare. They knew he wouldn't go—none of them sure would have gone, especially under the conditions it was placed!! And each one of them silently breathed a sigh of relief that they hadn't been the subject of today's dare. Besides, were they to be gone too long after dark and their folks become aware of it, there'd be hell to pay! That was almost guaranteed to be worth a good thrashing, in anybody's house!

Once he accepted the dare, Floyd grabbed his fishin' pole and the fish he'd caught to take home to momma; the rich mud felt good between his toes, but he had other things on his mind now. 'How in the world did I get myself into this one?' he mused. Each of the other boys as well made their way home, most of them needing to get the milking done for the night.

When Floyd arrived home, one thing he knew for sure—he wasn't gonna go alone! He might, just might, be able to talk his brother Lanzo into goin' with him. They could tell the folks they was goin' to a neighbors' for a couple hours and not to worry. But would Lanzo go? What if he did end up having to go by hisself? As these thoughts were turnin' round in his head, he heard Lanzo choppin' wood—the choppin' block was set off to the house a piece, so he could be sure and talk without bein' heard by Momma and the others. 'Hey Lanzo, come here fer a minute.' Lanzo, on hearing his younger brother's voice, left the axe, glad to have a reason to stop for awhile. As Floyd related the afternoon's events, Lanzo's eyes got big, and a mischievious smile crept over his face. 'They God Floyd, we do this and we alls be hee-ros from here on out!' With his older brother's confidence, he braced his shoulders and determined that this wasn't gonna be such a big thing after all.

What Floyd hadn't realized, is that Lanzo was not the only one listening—their second oldest brother, Isaac, was over by the pump and curious about what these two little rascals were up to, decided to listen in on the conversation without making his presence known...and boy was he glad he did!! Isaac was a prankster and, though serious by nature, loved to take advantage of any oppurtunity that presented itself to get a good laugh. Actually, this trait was not peculiar to him— seemed like sometimes all of Caney Fork was looking for a good reason to laugh. That's why funny situations and stories were rehearsed and told and retold year after year, adding to this hearty laughter that seemed to mark the Cooks. And now Isaac had his chance; his own plan immediately came together. He had to go down to the Ledbetter place anyway; he'd promised old man Ledbetter that he'd come by and take a look at their pump, that was getting harder and harder to draw up water. It wouldn't be too much farther to Judaculla Rock, and he'd be right there waiting for his younger brothers!

Darkness was just now falling—Floyd and Lanzo made their excuses to their folks after dinner, and quickly got on their way. Floyd especially wanted to get this over and done with!! Their thoughts were so tied into the rock however, that they fell into telling one story after another on the way there. They even talked about Granny Beck, the witch of Caney Fork!! Everybody knew her, and everybody also knew she had special powers—some said they were from God Almighty, but most of the community said they were straight from hell. They had even heard tell of a distant cousin whom Granny Beck had enchanted, right there at Judaculla Rock!! Folks said that he even made a 'pack' with the devil, and that he was never the same after that. And wouldn't you know, Granny Beck sometimes ventured out to Judaculla Rock at night, when no one suspected a thing, to do her 'coctions' and all kinds of other stuff!

They had walked a good long ways ('cause it's a long-ways walk from their home to Judaculla Rock) but far from being tired, both those boys were wired high!! They'd seen some of their neighbors along the way, and waved at all of 'em (except for cranky old man Hindershal, he never greeted anybody with a decent word!), never stopping to tell the reason for their journey.

Well, it wasn't far now, maybe half a mile or so. And by now it was pitch black...there was a bit of moonlight, but not a full moon, so it made it difficult to get back to the rock. They knew the way all right—it was a nice wide road that lead all the way back there. They were both secretly glad there *wasn't* a full moon, 'cause folks said that was when Grany Beck was sure to be there, and sometimes even turned into a horse!

There was nothing unusual about the night—nothing at all. The typical woods sounds were actually kind of comforting to these country-bred boys. They could hear the hoot-owls, announcing their presence, and also hear the quick flights of the many bats who came out in search of food. The creek was babbling in the background, and there were cows in the nearby barn, who were mooing with anxiety as they awaited their turn to be milked.

There it was...finally. They were only about 200 yards away. They had been talking quietly the whole way, but now their conversation became a bit more animated...'Lanz, I'll just go on and get that ol' rope,' said Floyd as he rushed ahead a bit. Lanzo just kind of tagged along. Just as he was about to grab the rope, with his heart beating furiously, there it was...he couldn't deny it. He thought he'd heard something, but quickly dismissed it to the back of his mind. But in the practical silence of the night, there was an unmistakable rustling off in the thicket to the left of the rock. Floyd froze. 'Lanzo, you hear that?' 'Y-y-y-es...I s-s-s-shore did.' They were paralyzed with fear just long enough to halt them in their tracks. Then all of the sudden, from that same place where the rustling was coming from, erupted this hideous, cackling laughter. 'Let's go!!' shouted Floyd as he grabbed the rope and bolted for the road. Lanzo tripped over a half-hidden stump as he too ran with all his might. That awful laughter increased, as well as the rustling in the woods, and it seemed to be following them, not too far behind. Once they were out onto the open road, they didn't stop to look behind, nor did they talk. But they ran and ran, for all they were worth, following the main road exactly the way they had come in. They were breathing so hard, they felt as if their hearts were in their throats, but no matter—they kept running. The dogs along the way, announced their arrival, with an assortment of howls and barks, that would have woken the dead. But no matter. They just kept running.

Finally about two miles down the road, with about a third of the way covered, they were sweating and breathing so hard, they just had to slow down to rest. They walked for about a half a mile and came up on a bend in the road, taking them up and around a hill. The kept walking at a fast clip, and all they could think about was getting home! Up to the left, there was a big, burned out stump, left over from one of Uncle Romalus' logging operations. Their nerves were so on edge, they stayed as far away from that old stump as they could. But all of a sudden, that same hideous cackling started low, and continued from right behind that stump!! 'JESUS' cried Floyd, and once again, both of them hot-footed it for home, this time they didn't stop for anything.

As they reached the curve that would carry them into the yard, and the safety of home, they finally slowed down. Neither one of them could talk, nor did they want to—that would be for later. They just needed to dip their heads 'neath the flow of water from the pump, and calm themselves down so's not to raise a ruckus with momma. 'This has been the wors' night a' my life,' thought Floyd, 'I'm never gonna back to that place again—even in the daylight!' The two of them spent a good while resting, and getting their wits together, and finally went inside to get to bed.

Morning came early as usual, and the family got up at sunrise. There were cows to milk and eggs to gather. Hogs had to be slopped, and there was plenty of work waiting out in the fields—seems like that hoeing and plowing and weeding never got done. But they knew that their very survival depended on their ability to keep at it, day after day.

Once their first chores were done, they came in for breakfast, and boy did it smell good this morning! His daddy often said "Theys nothin' that'll cheer a man's heart more'n a good breakfast," and his momma made sure they 'was plenty cheered.' Jim, their married oldest brother, had come by early, had some business to do with daddy in town, so the whole family were seated at the table, being served with those big, steaming plates of biscuits and gravy.

Isaac seemed to have a lot of energy this particular morning—he usually took his time in 'wakin' up.' But he had a mischievous grin on his face, that he had trouble hiding. 'What's got you'all lookin' like a cheshire cat?' quizzed their daddy. 'Oh, nothin' in particular,' he replied. 'I was jus' kina curious 'bout where these two bear cubs was at las' night.' Floyd and Lanzo looked at each other, and were actually glad for the chance to spill it all out—even if it might mean a whippin' for lying to momma and daddy.

First Floyd started, and then Lanzo interjected...and their eyes were as big as saucers as they told about the biggest 'skir' they'd had in their lives! The younger ones were mesmerized by the audacity of their older siblings, and didn't even move as they hung on every word. Ethan and Artie, their folks, didn't know what to make of it all. Finally when they had finished, and were looking at the floor ashamed, Isaac let out a laugh that shook the whole house...it was more than a laugh!! He had tears running down his cheeks and couldn't even talk for a few seconds. 'Jus' what's so funny?' Floyd asked angrily. Once Isaac got himself composed, he said, 'Now just what did that witch's cackle sound like—something like this?' And with that, he repeated the same eery sounds he had made the night before. Floyd jumped to his feet.."What?...I mean..how did you...you mean to tell me...were you there?" Once again his innocent questioning sent Isaac into rales of laughter again. 'You want to see your witch of Judaculla rock,?' he pleaded. 'You's lookin' at him.' With that the whole family joined in the laughter, except for Floyd and Lanzo. It didn't take too long though, before Lanzo saw how funny it was. Their momma was laughing so hard, she was slappin' her sides, throwin' her head back, and howled like he hadn't heard her in a long time. With him being the only hold-out, Floyd couldn't hold back either and joined in with their glee. 'I really gotchee this time,' said Isaac. 'Yeah, I reckon,' agreed Floyd. 'But at least I got this,' and with that, he reached down behind the potato box and brought up his prized rope. 'Well, I think we've all had our fun,' said momma, wiping her eyes with her apron. 'Let's just let this pass by, and be our little family secret.' With nodding heads and work to be done, they got up from the table and got on with their day.

But that didn't keep his momma from chucklin' all day long!

"...A CUNNING HUNTER, A MAN OF THE FIELD..."

Chapter 3

The great love of Floyd's life was hunting—it was at the very least the weekly chore of all the men in Caney Fork, if not more often, and for most, it was much more than an obligation to put food on the table. Jackson county during the 19th century was abundantly blessed with a great deal of wildlife, which readily served to supplement their diet. Deer, bear, coons, squirrels and wild turkeys were thick in the area, and in fact, folk were hard pressed to keep up with these critters so they could bring their crops in. It was a challenge to keep them thinned down enough, so they'd not eat their sweat-born crops, or attack their domestic animals, usually their chickens, geese or hogs. So every boy, as soon as he could walk, was trailing his pa, his uncles and/or his grampa, learning the lay of the land and obtaining the wisdom of the ages on handling guns, knives and once in awhile, bow and arrow.

But there was no doubt about it—Floyd's favorite game was squirrel-hunting. From the smallest of tykes he was fascinated by these noisy, nervous, fat, quick creatures. He also quickly learned to love his momma's squirrel stew, which was a special favorite of the family, even though it was served often.

Floyd's pa had taught him well on how to use a gun, and with three older brothers itching to get a good shot in any time they could, there was plenty of company to keep on their countless hunting trips. Pa had rules about hunting that his boys knew better than to break; first of all, you had to be at least thirteen before you started hunting by 'yo'sef.' And even then, it was better to go with somcone older. There were just too many things that could happen in the woods. Secondly, all your chores had to be done first—twarn't even no sense in askin' to go if yer chores weren't done! And third, you had to be back before dark. Floyd's pa Ethan was born just shortly before the 'Indian removal' and he had grown up hearing lots of Indian stories, some of them first-hand from the Indians themselves. Though they were all either scattered to the farthest hills or out west by the time he became a young man, there was bred into him a healthy respect for the wilderness, and the many unknowns that could sneak up on a man without him knowing it. He made sure he passed this on to his sons, but he wasn't always too sure that they paid him a whole lot of mind when it came to his huntin' rules.

Floyd's gun was an old 22 that had been handed down to him

by his brothers, one that they had all learned to shoot with. The older they got, the more opportunities they had to wheel and deal, and each one of them had some way or another gotten himself a better gun. Mind you, none of them were new...when someone got a new gun on Caney Fork, it was news that was sure to bring all the menfolk down to admire it. And it was never a young man who got a new gun—it was always an older man who had skimped and saved, or had happen to fall on a piece of luck. A new gun for a young man was a dream he'd have to wait a l-o-n-g time to fulfill. But no matter—as long as it worked, that's what counted to Floyd. And at any rate he had developed a kind of affection that only a born hunter understands, for his little old 22.

Floyd seemed to have a real knack for knocking off squirrels as well. His gaze was steady, as well as his arm and the times were rare when he came home without a bag full of squirrels for momma to skin and cook up. Knowing how much work she and the girls had to do, he often did the skinning himself, even though it *was* woman's work. The pelts he would clean and stretch out to dry and cure, and he'd find lots of uses for them. Once in awhile if it was especially a nice, big one, and if the shot had come off as he'd planned, he could even use the pelts as a type of currency, mostly with his friends who never could seem to keep up with Floyd's hunting skills. Even his older brothers would have had to admit to a bit of jealousy, but they managed to keep it to themselves, and let Floyd bask in his glory and hunting fame.

It didn't take long at all for Floyd to figure out his favorite routes—he had several of them, and as observant as he was, seemed to always know where the biggest and best squirrels spent their time. He almost always went with someone else, not only because he wanted to respect his daddy's wishes, but that was part of the whole fun of it, being able to take someone along, talking and laughing. Sometimes he would still go with his older brothers, but more and more often, he would incline for his younger cousins, neighbors or friends his own age. He was rapidly developing a reputation as a skilled hunter, and most other boys were thrilled to go out on a hunt with Floyd Cook.

One particular fall Saturday, Floyd had finished early with his chores, and had been itching ever since he woke up, to go up on the ridge squirrel hunting. Winter was coming on, so the squirrel's were gonna be a bit harder to find. According to that year's Farmer's Almanac, it promised to be a cold winter too, and even as a teenager, he felt the weight of responsibility on his shoulders for the rest of his family. Everyone of them had their own work, and he had taken squirrel hunting as part of his. He didn't want his family going hungry on account of him!

He yelled across the way to the nearest neighbor, and two of the boys were there in no time, each one carrying his own hand-me-down. They were both shotguns, which Floyd disliked for squirrel hunting, but that was all they had, and the matter wasn't even discussed. So they took off early that brisk afternoon, each one with his empty burlap bag strung over his shoulder. As a youngster, this moment would have been one to bet, and to see who would bring the most back home. But the other boys, as well as Floyd, knew that it was pointless to enter into this kind of game. Floyd always brought the most home—he didn't want to make them feel bad by losing; nor were they up to challenge the one who, without question, was the 'squirrel hunter' of the valley. At least as far as their age group went. So the matter was left, and they began to hike up the mountain.

After about an hour, Floyd had bagged three squirrels, all with clean shots that didn't damage the bodies. His two neighbors had bagged one each, but having used shotguns, the shot was scattered in a couple different parts of the squirrel, and it was going to be a challenge to clean them up enough to make a meal. But at least they got one. The afternoon was still young, and they kept moving along the trail that all of them knew so well. Floyd's grampa still came up in these ways, and always had a story to tell along the way. He found himself missing the old man and wishing that Grampa Hence would've come along with them on that day.

The further up the mountain they went, the clearer and stronger the air became. Each of them inhaled deeply and revelled in the experience. There were a lot of mountain flowers still blooming, and Floyd felt this must be a little piece of heaven, surely. The chirping and squawking of the birds throughout the forest, and the never-ending chatter of those squirrels, beckoned them to continue their journey. It seemed like every ten or fifteen minutes, Floyd would stop, motion for silence, and once again have another trophy for home. Most of those squirrels were gray or blue—put him in mind of the past war and he wondered how they all got along so well, when there was still so much bitterness between the Rebs and the Yankees. But all of the sudden out of the corner of his eye, not too high up in that hickory tree, was a red flash. It wasn't often that he could bag a red squirrel— local superstition said that red squirrels were bad luck, and it was best to just leave 'em be. But Floyd didn't pay much heed to superstition, and he could already envision the use he'd have for that pelt. He raised his gun, gazed down the barrel and waited until that ol' squirrel was distracted, filling his cheeks with nuts. He pulled the trigger and before he knew what hit him, that big red squirrel had fallen to the forest floor with a thud.

It had been two or three hours, and they all got what they came for. Floyd's bag was full, his neighbors' about halfway, and he decided to himself that along the way he'd give them a couple squirrels to balance out their take. He had a big heart, and he was happy to share what he had, whether it was squirrels, friendship, time or whatever. He knew he'd have to be a little diplomatic as well, so as not to hurt their pride, but that was another area that was being polished as he grew older, and his friends thanked him for his kindness.

Once they decided to turn around, they realized that they had gone further than they'd intended. They weren't worried about getting lost, but it had been a long time since they'd gone so deeply into the woods on the ridge. And another thing they'd noticed—apart from the squirrels they had bagged, they hadn't seen any other game! Not a fox, not a deer, not even a coon when they passed along the creek bank. Now that was odd; especially being here so deep in the woods, they ALWAYS saw something else. But today was different. Lots of squirrels, but nothing else.

They continued on down the mountain path, and stopped to rest a bit. One of the neighbor boys began to tell a joke on his brother that sent Floyd howling with delight!! The other one sulked a bit upon having his foolishness discovered, but the more Floyd laughed, the more he loosened up and soon was joining in the laughter with them. You couldn't be around Floyd Cook too long and remain serious. He seemed to have a knack of finding the humor in almost anything.

They got up to leave, when Floyd noticed an odd tone to the chatter of the squirrel overhead—it seemed to be a kind of scolding, rather than the typical 'squirrel talk.' 'Listen,' he said, and he motioned for his companions to be silent. They heard a thrashing in the brush up ahead, and all of a sudden that pungent, unmistakable musky odor that preceded its source. A bear!! They were upwind from it, so it hadn't detected their presence yet—but it certainly wouldn't be long. 'F-f-l-o-y-d,' stammered the younger of the two brothers. 'W-w-h-a-t are we g-g-g-o-n-n-a do?' He motioned for them to be quiet and to make sure their guns were loaded and ready. He'd only a few bullets left himself, and wondered how well a 22 and a couple of shotguns would do against this bear! He didn't know how big it was, but by the smell of it, it could be as big as an elephant!!

They decided to continue slowly, working their way down the trail, although that was bringing them closer to the bear's rummaging through the brush. They couldn't very well high-tail it through the woods, because in addition to being thick with underbrush where they were, it would certainly call attention to their foe.

By now they could hear the grunting and growling of this unwelcome intruder into their happy day. It sounded like he was ripping through an old log, probably having found an ant colony or a bee hive full of honey. But they weren't the least bit interested in finding out which was the case! The trail stretched before them winding and curving down the mountainside, and it was a clear shot, should they decide to run. But it was also a clear path for the bear, who could certainly outrun them. Floyd noticed that of his two friends, the younger one was quite nervous—in fact, he was at the point of tears. His older brother seemed fine with the whole situation, probably having been out on a bear hunt with his pa before. They silently made their way down the path, hoping with every step that their luck would hold out.

They seemed to be pulling it off—the bear had not changed her position nor redirected her attention, and kept at whatever she had at hand, that is, until the younger neighbor boy finally got so spooked that he started running. As he broke free from their predicament, he was able to hold on to his gun but his squirrel sack fell along the wayside. His brother followed him, feeling more a sense of responsibility towards him, then fear, but their sudden bolt, obliged Floyd as well (who was the last one in the line) to run after them. The other two had made quite a distance, when the younger boy tripped over a log in the trail, accidentally triggering his shotgun. The sound echoed throughout the woods, and as he struggled to his feet again, with his brother and Floyd hot on the trail behind him, that's when the bear appeared! He figured it was a sow, and from what he'd heard through the years, that could mean that she had cubs nearby. She wasn't huge, but when she stretched out, she was at least six feet tall—taller than the tallest of them!! She lumbered out onto the trail, pointing her nose in the air and emitted a low gurgling growl. She had caught full wind of the boys, had heard the shotgun go off, and was now wandering down the trail towards them. "GO!" shouted Floyd and they didn't have to be told twice. All three of them ran for all their hearts were worth, but not before Floyd had picked up the squirrel bag his young friend had dropped. The bear was still trying to figure out who these intruders were in her domain, and continued after them at a slow pace. But then she caught wind of something else, something more tantalizing, and she too began to run after the boys. Floyd was continually watching behind himself as he ran, and could see that the bear was gaining ground. He knew very well that his aim under these conditions would not be on target, and even though he'd accompanied his older relatives on bear hunts before, he'd never actually shot a bear and didn't know where to shoot! He figured it should be the head, but what if his little ol' 22 didn't pack enough power? What if he just succeeded in making her madder than she already was? By now, the youngest boy was yelling for all he was worth, and certainly scaring off any other creature that was within five miles, but unfortunately it wasn't working with the bear. Suddenly Floyd had an idea—he'd throw back his friend's squirrel bag, and maybe that would distract her long enough to put sufficient distance between them, so that they could get away. So at once he gave it a good thrust, directly behind him, and those juicy morsels landed right at the bear's feet. Her sense of smell was keen however, and she came to an immediate stop. As she examined the contents of that bag, she ripped it open with a swipe of her pa and began to feast on what would have been tomorrow's supper for those neighbor boys. While she gorged herself on this unexpected delicacy, those three boys continued running until they got to an open field at the bottom of the mountain. They crossed it, heading towards home, and when they could see that the bear was nowhere insight, they slowed down to a quick walk. When they finally got their wind again, Floyd said, 'I jus' wish I woulda had pa's bear rifle with us'—we'd a been chewing on bear sausage all winter.' His youngest friend just said, 'All I want is to get home,' and with that they made their way home with another tale to tell.

"...IF ANY MAN BE IN CHRIST, HE IS A NEW CREATURE..."

Chapter 4

The spiritual life of the Caney Fork community had always been a priority, at least as long as anyone could remember. The Tuckaseegee Baptist Association, established in 1829, was born as the result of a tremendous revival that swept through western North Carolina, with many souls being brought into the kingdom of God, and many churches formed as well. There were two things that you didn't challenge in these parts—the moonshiners, and the Tuckaseegee Baptist Association, who obviously were at odds. The unrelenting tension produced by these opposite clamors for attention sometimes even came to blows. Many folk said that the 'Sociation' even had more authority then the law; one thing was for sure...they were here to stay, and they weren't about to relinquish not even one inch of hard-fought territory that had been wrestled from the devil and his likes.

In a place that had never seen a circus, where news from the outside world came more often by word of mouth than by any other form, the church services were a bright light, and an anticipated respite from the hard, never ending toil that every family had to endure. The Sunday services, which were for a long time just once a month, were simple, but powerful. The sermons of visiting preachers were strong exhortations to righteousness to 'let God have His way,' Almost every service could count on having 'mourners' come forward, repenting of their sins, and determined to surrender to the One who so lovingly beckoned.

But oftentimes, it must be said, the reason why the church house was so full, was simply that there was nothing else to do. Many times the teenagers would have rather been down at the fishin' hole (both girls and boys) but were forced to come along to church, to make sure their crooked paths were made straight. Therefore, sitting in the back, in the very last pews was the norm, and their entertainment was found, not only in the idiosyncracies of a particular preacher, but also in the folks that came to listen. This kept the deacons busy with an ever watchful eye, and a long 'taddlin' pole' that was often employed to set those younguns straight. One whack on the top of the head, or the back of the hands, was all it took to keep 'em quiet at least for the rest of that particular service. Each deacon had his peculiar fame and nickname with this age group, and it wasn't too uncommon for them to bet before going into service who would handle the pole, how many whacks he would give, and who would get the most.

It wasn't all fun and games though—several of those teenagers saw the sincerity of their parents, who lived at home the same they did at church. These consistent testimonies of simple, God-fearing people, did a great deal to maintain the gospel from generation to generation, and no one could deny the importance of the church, in times of crisis . Very few families had not lost someone to death— whether it was the war, or sickness, or an accident in the woods. Life and death were very intimately interrelated, which brought a sober tone and reality to Caney Fork's community.

Fall was a time of year that everyone looked forward to. It was first of all harvest time and even though it meant the hardest work of the year, it also meant a few new clothes, some extra treats to eat, and a breath of hope to make it though the long hard winters which were so common. So it wasn't long before this time of celebration also became synonymous with 'revival.' The churches of the whole county scheduled their revival services for the fall, and they were always the most exciting, noisy, blessed moments anyone ever had. Life came to a standstill by the time autumn rolled around, and if you weren't busy about harvest, you were certain to be in church.

A 'normal' revival service lasted two weeks, oftentimes three. This meant that every night of the week the whole family would make their way to the meetin' place. Sometimes simple 'brush arbors' were erected, to be used only for the revival and then dismantled. Other times it might be a barn, or other suitable place to hold the crowds. One thing was for sure, and that is you were gonna have a hard time finding a place to sit—seemed like the whole world came to revival.

The line-up of preachers that would come through on a regular circuit was a 'who's who' of regional religious figures. One in particular that was sure to bring in lots of mourners was the Rev. Furthermore Quint. He was a preacher man from over Tennessee way, and was a well travelled man, much in demand throughout this part of the south. He was a big man—some say he could swing an axe all day long chopping wood, and not even stop to rest before goin' out bear hunting, sure to bring in at least one before dark. He had a scar that ran from his forehead down to his jawline, a result of a Yankee saber during the war that should have killed him. Instead the experience, once he recovered, brought him to Jesus. Many men had turned to Christ during the war:

> *"...In the army of General Lee, while it lay on the upper Rappahannock, the revival flame swept through every corps, division, brigade and regiment...The suscepitibility of the soldiery to the gospel is wonderful, and doubtful as the remark may appear, the military camp is most favorable to the work of revival. The soldiers, with the simplicity of little children, listen to and embrace the truth. Already over two thousand have professed conversion, and two thousand more are*

penitent...Oh! It is affecting to see the soldiers crowd and press about the preacher for want of tracts, etc. He has to distribute, and it is sad to see hundreds retiring without being supplied."...(pg. 31) In the South, little seemed to be left <u>except</u> religion."
(Gardiner H. Shattuck, Jr. <u>"Revivals in the Camp"</u> Christian History magazine, Issue 33, vol. XI, no. 1, pgs. 29, 31. Published by Christianity Today Inc. PO Box 11618, Carol Stream, IL 60188

Rev. Quint never tired of tellin' how God had saved not only his life, but his soul and called him into the ministry as well. That scar gave an awesome impression, especially to the children—some actually ran away when they saw him! Although he was big and somewhat threatening, his heart and passion for the lost were evident, and he would stay for hours, 'prayin' through' with anyone who needed that kind of time. Preacher Quint was blunt, and didn't mince words, and that's why he was especially popular with the men. Although he had made many of them so mad they could spit, he also had a grace about him to draw them into the loving arms of a forgiving God.

So when it was announced in late summer, that Preacher Quint would be a'comin', it put the whole valley to buzzin.' Families worked extra hard to get the harvest in on time for the revival, 'cause no one wanted to miss, not even one night.

Floyd, as a budding young man, had somewhat gone along

with the ebb and flow of church activities. His folks had never been part of the church, and had little time for 'those hypocrites' that went 'all out.' There were enough of his cousins and friends as well, who had their own opinions about getting 'too high on the hog' about church, and he wasn't about to stir their mockery by pursuing his ever-present desire to know God more.

But things were changing with Floyd—he was now 20 years old, and doing some serious thinking about life in general and his future in particular. His much loved Grandpa Hence had died in February of this same year, leaving a great hole in Floyd's heart, and causing him to reflect on the brevity of life.

Floyd had never been one to back down from a fight, nor had he been slow to express his opinions. And this particular fall of 1885 seemed to bring together a lot of thoughts and feelings that had been floating around in his head for a long time. It was during what folks called an 'Indian summer'— one of those delightful extensions of summer that lasted until late September, sometimes even into October. It meant hot days and cold nights, but they were always welcomed, and understood as a token of God's favor before winter set in.

Revival was to start the next week—and Floyd observed a scene he had enjoyed so many times before as he was growing up. The men working the fields, the womenfolk canning and making sure their men were well taken care of. Even the children got involved, and each one of them had a special task to do; and failing to do so by 'dawdlin' was sure to bring a thrashin' with a hickory switch. But there wasn't often much of that—the kids had too much fun being part of something much bigger than themselves.

Floyd was feeling uneasy, and even depressed. Reconstruction had not turned out as had been hoped. The whole south felt betrayed by the federal government who, far from lending them a helping hand in getting started once again, seemed to punish the entire region because of the past war. If you wanted to get folks riled up, just start talking about 'Reconstruction' and you were sure to hear a harangue of at least an hour, by any and everyone that was within earshot. "That's why weze Democrats," they'd say. "All them ol' Filadelfia-lawyer Republican-type look out for is theirself." Unemployment was high, and many folks fretted about making it through winter. There was even a slow trickle, that would later turn into a genuine river, of immigration towards the west, out to Washington territory. Floyd had a few relatives who had ventured out that way and the few letters that had made it back home, brought glowing reports of opportunity in the woods. Nobody seemed to put much stock in this kind of news however, if only for the fact that it was looked on as a 'foolhardy' venture to go clear to the other side of the country. 'They God, that's clear out by the Pacific Ocean.' Floyd himself didn't pay too much mind, because he couldn't imagine leaving his family that he loved so dearly, and the only life he'd ever known. Nosiree...his place was in Caney Fork and it was there that he would live out his days.

Revival services got started on Sunday evenin' as they always did, and 'Lord a'mighty' did they sing, and stomp and shout. It seemed like the whole valley ached to have this spiritual release. Lots of folks 'got happy' and it was midnight before the last ones made their way home. Floyd had enjoyed himself as usual, but at the same time couldn't shrug off this deepening sense of despair. He hadn't sat in the back pews as he usually did, but had purposely made his way up towards the middle of the congregation, just to get away from those younger kids that couldn't seem to keep themselves quiet. They were constantly jabbing, poking, giggling and trying to avoid the 'on-duty' deacon, and he wanted none of that. He wasn't in the mood.

The nights carried on and seemed to grow in intensity—one night Nancy Aiken and some of the other womenfolk got so happy they started to shout and strut around the sawdust 'mournin' area' like a bunch of hens trying to escape a fox. They laughed and cried, and a couple of 'em even got so worked up that they fainted and had to be carried off to the side to get some air. It was all part of a tradition though, and though Floyd hadn't experienced a lot of this up close, it didn't feel foreign to him. He was glad that his people were able to have a little bit of happiness in the midst of poverty and depression that seemed to grip them at times.

Two weeks had gone by, almost every night seeing someone giving their hearts to Jesus, ususally right down at the mourner's bench in front, crying and bawling for all they were worth. This wasn't a strange sight atall for Floyd—he'd grown up with it. But what was stranger for him the last few nights, is that he found himself wondering what it was that they felt? Had he ever felt something like that? Was he even saved? It seemed like the preacher's words were hammering home to him a message he couldn't escape, and yet he didn't know what he should do about it all. He wasn't bad—he'd always been in church too. Many had said he was a good son, and his own folks sure found enough ways to express that. They were proud of their boy, and he'd never doubted their trust in him. So why did he feel so confounded and confused? He was a hard worker, and people loved to be around him, even the older ones—he had a way of telling stories that was sure to get a laugh. But now it was he who didn't feel like laughin.' What's happening to me?

This particular night, Floyd arrived late to the meetin'—he hadn't intended on it, but that old bull had gotten out again, and he had had to go chase it down, and bring it back inside the fence. Once that was done, the fence had to be repaired and by the time he'd gotten that all taken care of, his folks and brothers and sisters had already left for meetin.' Once he walked in, there was no place to sit—all the pews were taken, so he had to stand in the back, much as he disliked doing that. But he noticed right off, that every one of those fool teenagers were paying rapt attention to Rev. Futhermore Quint, and he was just gettin' started with his message.

Folks said that Furthermore got his name from the Bible—his mother, who'd been left a widow before he was born, was weighted down with the cares of the world. She had four4 little ones to raise by herself, and another one on the way, who was due any day now. One of the circuit preachers had come by and invited her to meetin' and so she gathered up her brood and as best she could, made her way to the meetin' place. It was while she sat listening to the preacher, and the text he used, that she knew what she was going to name her baby. With a voice shrill with authority, the preacher read from I Chronicles 29:1,

> *"Furthermore David the king said unto all the congregation, Solomon my son, whom alone God hath chosen, [is yet] young and tender, and the work [is] great: for the palace [is] not for man, but for the LORD God."*

She knew her baby was a boy, and she knew what she was going to name him. She could neither read nor write, and didn't really know what 'furthermore' meant, but she liked the sounds of it, and that was that. The next week when her baby was born, she put him 'Furthermore' for his name. It wasn't until after he himself was converted as an adult, that 'Furthermore' came to appreciate his name and the unique distinction it gave him wherever he went.

Floyd quickly became mesmerized by Rev. Quint—he seemed to be looking right through Floyd's confused heart, and the sweat began to bead up on the back of Floyd's neck. How does he know how I'm feeling? What is God telling him about me? The message continued from I Samuel 17:58,

"And Saul said to him, Whose son [art] thou, [thou] young man?"

The preacher's voice roared from the pulpit, and could be heard echoing throughout the woods. He knew just the right emphasis to give to the words, and was a master at his timing. After an intense exhortation, he would stop and look all around the congregation in silence. No one made a move, but there were slight murmuring sobs that could be heard starting among the womenfolk. Furthermore Quint knew mountain humor as well as the back of his own hand, and would intersperse a couple of stories that had happened that week, which broke the tension, and served even more to draw the entire crowd into his 'net.' Having given them a chance to laugh, he again returned to the main thrust of his message that night: *"Whose son art thou young man?"*

> "If you have not surrendered your life, your will and your future to the Lord God Almighty—if you've never been borned again—you're not a child of God. As good as your mommy and daddy have been to you, they can't make you a son of God. The Bible says in John 1:12 that *"as many as received him, to them he gave the power to BECOME the sons of God."*

With that the Rev. Furthermore Quint looked right directly at Floyd and said, "Young man, whose son art thou?" No one else seemed to notice because they were caught up in their own emotional involvement with the message, but Floyd felt that the eyes of the whole congregation were upon him. His knees grew weak, his heart was pounding wildly and he was dizzy—he thought he was going to pass out. And yet he was sure he was hearing the voice of God. Maybe this was the first time ever in his life, that he had heard God speak so clearly to him. All of the sudden, he understood what his struggle of the past few months had been—his depression, his hopelessness. He was not yet a son of God! All his life he'd heard about it, he'd seen people weeping and giving their hearts to Christ, but he himself had never actually taken that step. Why? Why had he taken this long? Maybe it's because he was turned off by the religious hypocrisy of some; seemed like some of those who shouted the loudest at revival, were the worst gossips around! It certainly didn't help that both his momma and daddy were so negative about church. But this was by no means all, because he had a great deal of respect for others who simply and humbly lived out their Christianity on a daily basis. But he couldn't stomach the hypocrites. Was it that that held him back? He didn't know—all he knew at this moment is that God was speaking to him and waiting for an answer. It wasn't only God either, it was no one less than Rev. Furthermore Quint!! In a split second he made his way down to the mourner's bench— there was already a neighbor lady rolling around in the sawdust, alternately moaning, shrieking, and then crying out to God for mercy. Floyd fell to his knees and began to pour out his heart to God. He asked for forgiveness for all of his sins; it seemed like he was seeing everything he'd ever done wrong brought before him. Each sin he remembered deepened his sense of uselessness, and his utter lost condition before a holy God. By this time, the whole altar was full of mourners, and there was shouting and praying the a holy pandemonium going on over the church. Young and old alike were being touched by the power of God, and Rev. Quint couldn't get around fast enough to pray with them all. When he finally made it to Floyd, he laid his big calloused hands on his shoulders and prayed at the top of his lungs for salvation. Floyd seemed transported to somewhere else, and wave after wave of joy began to wash over him. He was clean! He was forgiven! He was a child of God! Now he could answer Preacher Quint! The joy he felt bubbled up from deep within his heart and spilled over in an uncontrollable laughter that lasted for several minutes. Then he began to shout! Now he understood what they all had felt before!! He couldn't keep himself from shouting!! He wanted the world to know—"I'm a child of God!"

Long into the night their shouts, and laughter went on. A good part of the congregation began to sing some of their favorite hymns, and it seemed like this service was never gonna end. Oh the joy of it all! Rev. Quint gave Floyd a big bear hug and continued praying for him. Once he finished, he held him out at arms length, looked him straight in the eye and said, 'Son, keep the banner wavin.' *("He brought me to the banqueting house, and his banner over me was love." Song of Solomon 2:4, KJV)* With that Floyd let out a hoot, and slowly each family made their way home, mightily blessed by the presence of the Lord Jesus Christ. This phrase was to become Floyd's theme and 'calling card', and was what was to identify him above all else that he said and did for the rest of his life.

Every revival was always terminated with baptisms, and this was to be no exception. And what a glorious day that final Sunday was. The crowd was as big as it had been throughout the whole revival, and they made their way down to the 'baptizing hole,' most of them walking, but some in old wagons, or mounted on horses. It was a magnificent sight this parade, and there was to be a big picnic afterwards, so it couldn't be any better. As they moved along towards the river, they sang and some of the younger women who were just getting initiated into their mother's and aunt's mountain tradition, started to shout. Their joy was carried by the slight breeze that had come up, and all of heaven was surely joining with them, rejoicing.

One by one the new converts were immersed beneath the baptismal waters, and there was a host of them that day. When it came Floyd's turn, Rev. Quint smiled with a joy that couldn't be contained. He looked at this fine young man and knew that God had a special work for him to do. The saints continued to sing as Floyd entered the creekhole where the preacher was waiting for him. "I'd like to say a piece," Floyd said, also with a smile that spread from ear to ear. "You folks all knows me—I was born and reared here, and you all knows who I am...or who I was. But I'm here to tell ye that Jesus Christ burst into my heart like a locomotive the other night, and I ain't been the same since. I do believe He has got a right special work for me to do, and I hereby declare that my life is no longer mine. This here is my public testimony that I now live for Jesus, and yer gonna see a new Floyd Cook round these parts." There were shouts of 'amen,' and 'hallelujah' and 'say it boy.' He was literally trembling with excitement and could hardly contain the gurgling emotion he felt deep within his heart. Rev. Quint took him by his broad shoulders as Floyd looked up at the bright sun that was shining overhead. 'Floyd Cook, by the authority vested in me as a minister of the gospel of Jesus Christ, and upon hearing from your own mouth the words of your conversion, I now baptize you in the name of the Father, and of the Son, and of the Holy Ghost. Amen." And with that, he thrust Floyd neath those waters and when he came back up, Floyd was shouting and laughing, swinging his arms and kicking his legs. "Oh glory to God!" This was just the start of a life time of service to God, one that would have many adventures, joys and sorrows. It was just the following Sunday, that he was welcomed into the fellowship of the believers when he became a fullfledged member of Balsam Grove Baptist church.*[9 October, 1885 as related in his obituary published in the Jackson County Journal, March 4, 1921]*

"HE WHO FINDS A WIFE, FINDS A GOOD THING..."

Chapter 5

Floyd's life began to take on all the marks of manly responsibility, now that he accepted the Lord and joined the church. He seemed to abound with new-found purpose and as he looked towards the future, he knew he would soon be needing a wife.

Courtship on Caney Fork was no fancy affair, but it wasn't without its social rules—a couple of generations previous it wasn't uncommon at all for first cousins to marry. It was a sparsely settled area, opportunity for travel was minimal, and a mate had to be chosen from those who were available! But now conditions had changed a bit, the population was much greater, and marriage between first cousins (or closer) was looked down upon. But having said that, almost everybody in the valley was related as it was, and those who weren't joined by blood, were well known as friends and neighbors. So it was almost certain that the one you would spend the rest of your life with, was someone you'd grown up with and knew very well.

For some time now, there was a beautiful young gal down the way named Alice Parker. Actually her full name was Sarah Alice, but everyone called her Alice, from a little girl. She was 15 years old, but of marrying age, and her budding beauty was noticed by several of the young men. Alice's family had been in the area for a long time and were descended on her mother's side from Hugenots who had fled from France in the early 1600's to find religious freedom on the shores of Virginia.

"In sixteenth and seventeenth century Europe, the persecution of non-Catholics divided nations, towns, and even families. Many newly-converted Protestants were killed; many were forced to reestablish at least a face-saving and probably a life-saving commitment to the Catholic Church; and many others were forced to flee, sometimes openly, sometimes covertly, to other countries where their desire to seek God's will directly would be unchallenged.

"Protestants were known by many terms in various countries...The members of the Chastain family who became and remained Protestants were known as Huguenots, because of their French heritage...

"Dr. Pierre Chastain, Huguenot, refused to renounce Protestantism and chose rather to leave his native France, to begin a new life in the New World. Genealogist[s] believe it is from this man that most, if not all, of the Chastains in the United States descend.

(From Book VII, The Family of Martha Ann Chastain Ray)

By 1696, the Pierre Chastain family had fled from Charost across the Jura Mountains to Vevey, Canton Vaud, Switzerland to escape religious persecution. Sometime after September 1698, the family departed Vevey and was found at The Hague in The Netherlands (Holland). From there, the family moved to London, England where they remained a short time while Pierre became active in gathering together a group of French Huguenot refugees for colonization in Virginia. Pierre Chastain, his wife Susanne Reynaud Chastain and five children were among the group of 207 passengers who embarked from Gravesend, England on April 19, 1700 aboard the ship Mary and Ann of London. This ship arrived at the mouth of the James River on July 12, 1700. The group settled in Manakin, Virginia about twenty miles up the James River. The group was given a 10,000-acre tract of land south of the James in an area once occupied by the Monacan Tribe of Indians.

(Biography of Dr. Pierre Chastain, Pierre Chastain Family Association website: http://www.kopower.com/~jimchstn/

Many of the Chastains had maintained a deep appreciation for their religious heritage, which was expressed through the lives of the many ministers, song leaders, and active members they produced.

Alice's poppa, 'Billy' Parker, was a veteran of the Civil War, and kept a life-long limp as a result. He always had stories to tell about the war, and especially never tired of relating how he'd been shot twice, once through the body, and once in the head. His wounds more or less healed up, and upon returning from the war, he married twenty year old Jane Chastain. He also fathered eight children, though with every passing year, those old wounds took an increasing toll. He was a man of great strength, however, and therefore was highly respected among his peers. He and Floyd's momma were first cousins, so the families knew each other well.

It wasn't any surprise therefore, when Floyd started coming over to the house with increasing regularity. Alice was flattered by this new attention, but she was also lady-like and quite shy. Floyd would stop and talk awhile, first of all with her poppa and momma, while Alice looked on and listened with interest—there was always several of her younger siblings around as well, to make sure they didn't miss a single move. Once in awhile they would be left alone on the big porch, which Alice both longed for and dreaded. She didn't know 'xactly how to conduct herself, and now that Floyd's visits were two or three times a week, she could see where this was going. Sometimes she was left without words, and there were some awkward moments of silence. But Floyd didn't let that last long, and would always end up making her laugh. That Floyd Cook always seemed to see the funny side of things, and he was quick with his wit. Alice knew one thing: she was falling in love with this tall, swarthy cousin of hers.

Winter normally was slow and often boring. But it seemed that no more had the first snowfall come and gone, then the daffodils were poking up from the ground. Christmastime had been one of the best she had ever spent, mused Alice, 'specially cause Floyd had gone huntin' and brought over enough fresh killed squirrels to feed the whole family. It was almost like a reg'lar Christmas feast, like the ones they have up north that you heard about from time to time. Sure, they 'as 'po,' but that didn't keep them from enjoying life to its fullest. And one thing for sure, they ALWAYS had plenty enough to eat!!

Floyd had made up his mind—that Alice Parker was the one for him. He loved the way she was; as the firstborn girl in her family, she had quickly learned to take care of the younger ones, and he discreetly observed how she did so with a great deal of devotion and care. It wasn't a chore for her, as he had seen it become for other girls her age around the valley. He'd never seen a temper in this gal, and her sweetness and shy posture had conquered his heart. That settled it—he was gonna talk to Billy Parker, and let him know of his intentions. He had prayed about it, he felt peace and love in his heart, and he was a practical young man. He'd given his heart to Jesus, and now it was time for him to marry and start a family. The only thing left to do, was to ask for her hand.

It was a few days later in February when Floyd showed up again, and was happy to discover that Billy was tending the animals out in the barn. He made his way right out there, and once he said, 'hey,' he got right down to business. 'Billy,' he started, 'you knows I's been comin' round here for a spell, and well… it ain't been for not havin' something better to do. I done fell in love with Alice, and wants to marry her. Would you be obliged to give me your blessin'?' Billy thought he'd have some fun with his soon-to-be son-in-law, and feigned being mad. 'They God Floyd, she's a big help to her momma—and you know the missus ain't in too good a'health. I jus' don't know if we can let her go.' Floyd was silent as he tried to determine if Billy was talkin' seriously or jestin'. Finally a big smile crept across Billy's face as he said, 'But after all, they's plenty of others to take up where she leaves off.' He reached out his hand and shook Floyd's—Floyd breathed a big sigh of relief and laughed out loud. 'Well, get on now; you'd better go and tell her before I get a mind to do so myself!' With that Floyd spun around, and almost ran into the barn door in his hurry to get to the house.

Once inside, Alice had already prepared him some hot chicken broth and some biscuits. Her momma had busied herself with some mendin', and somehow had made sure the little ones were occupied with other things. She somehow

knew what today's visit was all about. It was just Floyd and
Alice in the kitchen. As Floyd hurriedly ate and swallowed,
he finally said, 'Alice...I ah...well...I don't know jus' how to
say this all, but uh...will you marry me?' Alice's face
flushed as her eyes quickly darted to see who was listening.
But her excitement was too great and she rushed towards
Floyd who was now on his feet. She threw her arms around
him and she said, 'Oh Floyd, yes! yes! yes!!' Her squeals of
delight opened up the floodgates of curiosity from her
brothers and sisters who seemed to come out of the
woodwork, and before they knew it, the whole family was
standing there watching them with great approval. Billy had
come in from the barn, and had his arm around his wife. His
little Alice was going to be a bride!!

They quickly decided on a date for the next month, and their
plans were made in a whirlwind. There wasn't a whole lot
a'plannin' to do anyway, so it was just a matter of gathering
a few things together to start their own new home. Floyd's
daddy had an old house on his property, and they'd have to
make some good time fixin' it up, to make sure it was nice
and snug for the newlyweds.

The big day came on March 11, 1886—the happy couple had
put on their best clothes and made the long trek into town.
They took with them the required witnesses, and sought out
the justice of the peace. They paid for their license, were
pronounced 'man and wife' by the law, and with Alice's
squeal of delight at her newly formed family, they headed
back home for their 'honeymoon.'

'Lord, you're so good to me,' thought Floyd. 'And I thank you for giving me a good wife, who will also be a good mother to my children. Keep us healthy Lord, and provide for all of our needs. And may we serve you with all of our hearts, until our dying breath.'

Once they got back home, both of their families, as well as the neighbors and lots of church folks, had come by to wish them well. After a bone-warming chicken dinner, with dumplings, green beans, canned tomatoes, okra, corn and mouth-watering bread fresh from the oven, they finished it off with canned peaches and more apple pie than anyone could eat. This was a real celebration!! Of course as poor as these tarheels were, it was a rare to lack for food. They might not have had much, but they didn't go hungry. What with all the canning done by the women folk, the hams and sausages that were cured to last throughout the winter, they ate good! "It don't get any better than this," thought Floyd.

It was getting dark now, and time to retire to their honeymoon cottage and future home. Amidst all the well wishes, they made their way out, and when they got to their very own porch, they heard some laughter out beyond the well. All the sudden there were firecrackers going off! Floyd threw open the door to the cabin, grabbed his rifle, and quickly shooed away his prankster kin by firing a couple of warning shots in the air. They ran off yelping like buckshot coyotes, satisfied that they had completed their duty by following the newlyweds, and letting them know that they hadn't forgotten them! Floyd then spontaneously lifted Alice up and carried her across the threshold. "This is our home now, Alice, may God bless us all the days of our lives." With that he kissed her and thus they started their 35 years of marital bliss.

William Floyd Cook's Family
Grace, Susie, Rev. William Floyd Cook, Will,
Eular, Lorena, Alice, John, Ben

"...THY CHILDREN LIKE OLIVE PLANTS ROUND ABOUT THY TABLE..."

Chapter 6

Nobody ever thought about planning for a family—the children that came along, well those were the ones that God gave you. So there wasn't even anything to discuss; plus, the more children you had, the more help you'd have in the house and around the farm, so the birth of a baby always was an occasion for great joy. It wasn't but a month after their marriage, that Alice announced to Floyd that she was 'in a family way.' "Hallelujah!" he yelled as he picked her up in his arms and threw her in the air. God's blessings over them just continued to increase, and their hearts burst with gratitude.

It was January of the following year, that Alice's pains started and Floyd made a beeline for the midwife. He had no idea what to do, and he wanted to make sure everything turned out the way it was supposed to. It wasn't long a'tall before he was back with the midwife, and shortly after their arrival, both of their mothers, as well as aunts, other cousins and neighbors were coming by to see what they could do to help. As joyful a time as it was, it was also a very risky time, as there were no guarantees as to how things would turn out. The many local graves attested to the high incidence of young mothers and babies who had died in childbirth, so everyone was on red alert! Many of the women began to pray and intercede before heaven, crying out to God for the safety of both mother and child. Floyd decided it would be better to let them on with this women's work, and to go out by himself and pray. This was all new to him, and even though his faith had grown in the last year since he had given himself to Jesus, he was still plenty scared.

After having spent a good while in prayer, and feeling the peace of God, he kept himself busy with work around the barn. His hands were occupied in everyday tasks he knew by heart, but his mind was in there with Alice, praying under his breath for the safety of them both. Did he want a boy or a girl? It don't matter much to me, he thought. That's all in the Lord's hands—'Father, I just want them both to be all right.'

They'd been in the house about four hours, with Floyd making sure that he didn't go far. As nervous as he was, he must have worn a trench between the barn, and the pump, and the house, and then the barn again. Alice's groans could be heard from quite a distance, though they were low and muffled. Finally, she let out a scream that seemed to shake the very support timbers of the barn. This was followed by a slap, and a cry to match Alice's. It's over, he thought, and as he made his way to the house, his mother-in-law called out, 'Floyd Cook, come and see this new youngen the Lord's given you.' He trotted towards her, bounded into the house, and was presented with a little bundle, already cleaned up and wrapped in a receiving quilt made by a relative. 'Yous got you a little girl, Floyd.' 'Glory be,' he said with wonder. He made his way over to his wife, grinning from ear to ear, and as he sat beside her in the bed, he raised his voice in prayer, thanking God for His blessings. They later named her Lorena Isabella, who quickly learned to wrap her daddy's heart around her finger like a ribbon. She favored her momma a great deal, and as she grew Floyd could see his beloved wife reflected in their little girl more and more.

Lorena was three years old when the next one came around, and had been well prepared by her momma to give him the best welcome a baby could have. William Ethan was born in March of 1890, and sometimes it was hard to see who was mothering him more, his momma or his older sister. She was absolutely fascinated by this 'live doll' and begged her momma to hold him, to feed him, change him... anything she could do, just to be able to touch him. Will from the beginning had a disposition like his daddy's, and charmed the world from the start.

Grace followed next, born when Lorena was seven and Will, four. She was the picture of sweetness—all of the hassle her mother had borne in carrying her evaporated when she saw that cherubic little face. For that reason, Floyd and Alice chose 'Grace' as her name, because it seemed to so aptly describe this child's arrival.

Next in line was Ben—this pregnancy was difficult, following so closely on the heels of the previous one. Alice often had to lie down in the middle of the day, and was plagued by nausea and dizziness for a long period of time. She complained of feeling weak a lot, and had to rely on her older children more than ever to care for her newborn son Ben. Lorena once again assumed her role as surrogate mother. Will wanted to know how soon he was going to be able to walk and run, so he had to learn some patience before he could pull Ben along in his activities.

Eula ('Eud') showed up two years later...his birth was a difficult one, and the longest labor that Alice had had to date. The midwife was quite worried as she was tending to Alice, and sent word to the praying ladies to double their time, as this was gonna be a tough one. After a long, exhausting labor, their fifth child was finally born. From the very beginning he seemed to have a bit more of a competitive character than his brothers and sister, and was more demanding of everyone's time. Once again, Lorena was a great help to her momma. Will, by this time had growing interests, and was drawn more outdoors; Grace was the little princess of the family, but Ben was still close by and for a time had a certain jealousy that often results from two siblings of the same sex who are born close together. Ben's calm nature was often exasperated by the competitive and demanding expressions of his younger brother, but it wasn't long till that same tension was transformed into a closeness that was shared for the length of their lives. Eud also quickly became the family clown and jokester, and loved to get people to laugh.

Susie was next in line, and after three boys, Alice and the girls were thrilled to have another woman in the house to balance things out a bit!. Even though Lorena was now fourteen years old and already with thoughts of her own about raising a family, she readily gave herself to caring for this little jewel who came to live with them. Susie was the easiest baby to care for to date, and quickly slept through the night. She also was not colicky to the delight of her parents. Her coos and gurgles entertained the whole family constantly.

John Lewis followed two years later in 1903 and fit right into a well established family routine. His birth shortly after harvest, as well as revival, was taken as a promise of God for future abundance. This child had a set of lungs on him, that he put to work right away, and if he wanted something, there was no doubt in anyone's mind who it was that was asking!

Their last child was Paul, born in 1905...he brought to eight the number of children God had given to Floyd and Alice, and their hearts were bursting with gratitude for His goodness. At the same time, now shouldering the responsibilities of so many mouths to feed, the burden was much greater. Time was less, and life seemed to take on a more serious hue. But in the strength of the Lord they would go forward, trusting him with their health, their provision, and most importantly, to make their family a witness of the mercies of the Living God.

With their family now complete, each member continued to form his or her own personality and character. And under Floyd and Alice's watchful, strict, and godly eyes, they grew up in the fear of the Lord. There were times when that wasn't good enough though, and in those occasions, the fear of momma's hickory switch or daddy's horse strap would do the trick! They selected their "weapons of warfare" very skillfully, and were deeply committed to completing Proverbs 22:15,

> *"Foolishness is bound in the heart of a child; but the rod of correction shall drive it far from him."*

There wasn't one of their children who didn't believe that, and all had ample experience to back it up...some more than others. They learned quickly that momma and daddy meant business, and there was no foolhardiness when it came to obeying them, or obeying what the Good Book says.

They were a very loving and close family however; both Floyd and Alice loved each other deeply, and were quick to show it. Their hugs and kisses were daily fare. That loved spilled over onto their children as well, and they strove to express that love equally. These siblings maintained a deep love for one another all their lives, having learned early on—

from their momma and daddy's example, not only with them, but with friends, neighbors and other relatives—what really matters in life

Lorena naturally fell into a second mother's role, modelling Alice in so many ways. And it was good she did, as it would fall upon her and Will, a great deal of the raising of the younger ones. Alice and Floyd would spend long hours out in the fields, and they were left in charge. This could be a factor in her marrying relatively late, at twenty six.

Will, their oldest son, seemed to be blessed with the spiritual giftedness of his father, for he too, 'saw' or 'foresaw' things. People didn't take lightly when Will Cook said he had a dream, or had a vision— it was sure to come to pass.

Grace lived up to her name, and her sweetness was known far and wide—she was also very spontaneous and expressive in her love for Jesus, taking after her daddy, and it wouldn't be two minutes into the service when often she'd be shouting.

Ben was destined to share the spiritual zeal and passion of his father; as a young man, he too, felt the call to preach and quickly was trailing Floyd in learning all he could about what would be his life's profession. He loved to hear his daddy preach!!

Eula ('Eud') was caught in the pull between the older kids, and the younger ones—the inevitable struggle for identity for one caught in the middle—as well as between the ways of the world, and the ways of the Lord. Many tears were shed by Floyd and Alice over this headstrong and wayfaring son, who would marry the first time, father a child and divorce between the years 1920 and 1924. His was the life of the prodigal son. He too would become a preacher later on in life, but one that was not always approved of by his exacting older brother Ben, in spite of Ben's deep love for him.

Susie early on showed her inclination to help and to serve—in her quiet, unassuming way, her greatest joy was in helping others. She would become Caney Fork's midwife, responsable for the safe delivery of over two thousand babies over a forty year period.

As a youngster John loved to sing! He would delight his family with his spontaneous joyful song, and would really cut loose in church. Later on in life, that wonderful baritone voice would serve to inspire many in praising God. ,He would throw back his head, and with abounding joy, sing of his love for the Saviour.

And that leaves us Paul, the baby of the family. Somewhat abandoned by the busy lives of his parents, he was doted on by most of his older siblings, and would grow up with a quiet and shy nature.

William Floyd Cook

"...HE COUNTED ME FAITHFUL, PUTTING ME INTO THE MINISTRY."

Chapter 7

Floyd's conversion and subdequent baptism in water, only marked the beginning of a life-long pursuit of God. There were several things that reflected this—the first and most predominant was an insatiable thirst for the word of God. In every spare moment that he could find, Floyd was reading his Bible. The Word of God seemed to take on a life of it's own, and Floyd couldn't get enough of it. At almost every sermon or lesson, he would always have questions for the preacher, and would continue until he was satisfied with the answer. Another big change that took place in his life is that he was in the church house every time the doors were opened. Before, he had attended special services once in awhile, revivals, etc. but now he was often the first to arrive, and the last one to leave. Without being asked, he would make sure the stove was fired and stocked up with a good supply of cord wood. He would take a broom and sweep up every last bit of dust and dirt. He was tireless in his attendance to the house of God, and was the most happy when there.

The preacher and deacon board, observing the constant service that Floyd offered, recognized God's hand over this young man. So it was just two years after his conversion and baptism, that he was officially ordained a deacon in Balsam Grove Baptist church on 6 Oct 1887. *[Jackson County Herald, Sylva, NC 4 March 1921]* And that just added fuel to the 'far'! Given that he was now a married man, and a father on top of that, didn't leave any extra time atall!. But Floyd didn't let any grass grow under his feet—and thankfully he had a godly, patient wife who soon became accustomed to his constant activity, especially for the Lord.

Another big change in Floyd was his bold witness that he gave for Jesus—and it wasn't long atall before he started having results! His brothers and cousins began to respond with more interest in church, and some of his friends also accepted Jesus as their Saviour. Simultaneously though, there were some who were not so happy about all the changes going on in Floyd Cook, especially when he took 'hit 'pon hisself' to preach to them! And his first and most vehement opposition came from his own folks—they were bothered enough about his 'scan'lus' conversion, but their anger increased with his increasing devotion to the church. Both Ethan and Arty Cook were known to cuss like sailors, and their newly converted son became the most recent target for their tirades.

The target of Floyd's evangelistic efforts quickly became the moonshiners, some of whom were his relatives. For the most part they just listened, razzing him a bit, but there were a couple who got down right fired up! And told him 'flat' to stay out of their lives and 'bizness.' But to Floyd it 'twas no mind; they was los' sinners, and he'd just have to pray more for 'em, that's all. But he wasn't about to hold back on what he thought about that 'devil's juice' and where it was leadin' 'em all—straight to hell. These seeds would spring up later, and cause some real headaches for Preacher Floyd.

Anything they asked him to do, Floyd was right there. He began teaching a Sunday school class for boys, that became very popular with this age group. Sometimes he would take those same boys and go 'visitin' the old folks who were shut-in and couldn't get out to shout! It wasn't too long before he had a regular circuit, and the people waited for him anxiously. If Alice was too busy to go with him, once in awhile he'd be able to convince her to let Lorena go along with him on these visits. She soon learned to love those rare moments of accompanying her poppa, as he 'tol the folk about Jesus.' He would always make sure he prayed before he left their homes as well, and his bold, voluminous prayers soon became a familiar sound throughout the valley of Caney Fork.

One thing that Floyd especially enjoyed were the 'All Day Sings and Dinner on the Grounds.' They were programmed at least four times a year, but sometimes they would have smaller, informal type 'sangs' to hold 'em over until the big one came around. Folk would come from even the next county to partake in these little tastes of heaven, and it was a joy to behold! They truly were all day affairs, often times the folks would come prepared to spend the night, rigging up their simple canvas tents, or bedding down for the night in their wagons. They had their favorite places for the 'sangs' and one of them was a huge open field that Farmer Jones was only too happy to open up for the event. The field was situated such that it was up on a ridge—with natural acoustics that any professional singer would have envied. People would start to arrive even before breakfast time, get everything arranged, and would sing and eat, and eat and sing, and then sing some more. Their simple mountain melodies would echo out through the forests, mountains and valleys, and the people would be totally captured by their heavenly praises.

Everybody would have their turn at an 'All Day Sing'...it was true that they had a program, but it could always be adjusted for last minute groups or singers that showed up. And ususally, there was some local talent who would be too shy to sign up, but at the last minute would summon enough courage to go before the folks and sing their hearts out.

These 'All Day Sings' were not only inspirational but therapeutic—hard times were a constant theme especially for the folks of Caney Fork. Between sicknesses, deaths, unemployment, illicit relations, and a poverty that was fed by a lack of education, many needed an outlet or release from the pressure and tension caused. So it was also normal to see and hear folks get 'caught up' or 'fall out'...or 'shout till there was no more shout left.' For a people that didn't have much, to be able to partake in these spiritual and social feasts was just what the doctor ordered, giving them hope and strength to go on. And that's why they were so incredibly popular—the crowds would always have hundreds in attendance. (Of course it didn't take too many families to reach that number, taking into consideration that the average family size was at least ten!)

There was one particular All Day Sing that people talked about for years to come. It happened one spring day close to the end of the 19th century. Folks had been closed in for months during an especially cold winter, and many were ready to go 'stir-crazy.' Springtime was always a welcome relief, but especially this year, and therefore the All Day Sing was looked forward to with a great deal of anticipation. Floyd was on the planning and programming committee, and so had been extra busy in the weeks preceding the event, making sure all the details were taken care of.

True to custom, people started showing up about eight o'clock in their wagons, some on foot and many carrying guitars, mandolins or fiddles. They no more than got the platform set up, and pretty soon folk started getting situated, tuning and fine tuning their instruments. There was a real sense of expectation in the air, like something special was going to happen—and they weren't to be disappointed. There was a good group of folk off to one side, already praying for all they were worth, calling heaven down to visit them.

Floyd was bouncing around between the prayer meetin', attending to his family, and making sure the program was all set to go. The program was more an order of business, as no one cared about time; one group or quartet would sing until they got tired, and another would take up where they left off, while they went and got something to eat.

Things had gone well for the first couple hours, with the presence of the Holy Ghost descending upon these hungry people, and filling them up with love and hope. Sister Laura Blanchard had gotten so blest that she let out a shout that some thought at first was a hog call! Then she started to run! The more she ran, the more she shouted. She'd run one way, and then the next, eyes closed, her fists tight and thrown into the air as she'd go! She kept up her shoutin' finally running in a big circle that surrounded the platform. What she didn't see was a stick that was partially embedded in the ground, and as she ran, her foot caught that stick and threw her to the ground with a thud! But no mind! She just kept shoutin,' lost in glory as she lay on the ground for a good while. Some of the men got tickled as they had watched this sight, and themselves started to shout...but content to stay right where they were!

It was shortly after this incident, that Charley Weaver showed up—he was somewhat of an outcast of the community He'd been left an orphan at an early age, and grew up with his uncle and aunt. But their own family was so large that Charley never seemed to feel right about it, and as soon as he was able, he got out on his own. He lived in a little abandoned hunter's cabin in the woods, working odd jobs here and there, but often was drunk. Sad to see this in such a young man, and boy could he get wild! That's why people kept their distance when they saw him coming, 'cause they didn't want trouble. The children always ran from Charley, as he was the subject of their momma's nighttime threats to get to bed or 'Charley Weaver will get ye!' So when Charley showed up at the sing, there was a noticeable change, with children staying a bit closer to their parents, and the women folk wondering how to respond. The men didn't have much of a problem with Charley, and several had tried to sustain somewhat of a friendship with him over the years. But as reclusive as he was, it wasn't an easy task. But now here he was, and apparently sober. When Floyd assessed the situation, he decided to intervene immediately: 'Charley, welcome!! Are ye hungry? Let's get ye somethin' to eat!' and with that grabbed him by the arm and ushered him over to his own family's little site. 'Alice, let's get Charley fixed up.' Alice got to putting a plate together for him and outdid herself with her graceful expression of genuine love and compassion. Charley didn't say much but was obviously grateful for something to eat and the warm expressions of kindness that he rarely received. He sat down on a stump they pulled up for him, and the family as well as the whole camp went about their business.

It was after the Harkness Brothers sing, that Charley seemed to be paying particular attention. By this time there was a nice sun that had come through the early morning clouds, and you couldn't have wanted a better day. Anna 'Lar'

Parker got up to sing, accompanied by her brother Ralph on his mandolin, and the sweetness of heaven seemed to permeate the whole camp site. She started off, "I come to the garden alone," and all heaven cut loose! There were shouts from the men, women, and even some of the young ones were drawn away from their play and began to enter in to the rapture of the moment. Anna Lar continued: "And He walks with me, and He talks with me, and He tells me that I am His own" and on that note, she couldn't stand it anymore and cut loose with a little tarheel stomp...'Bless you Jesus! Thank you Lord! Oh I praise you my sweet Jesus!' While Anna Lar was in the midst of her glory fit, Charley Weaver couldn't stand it anymore—he'd been trembling ever since she started to sing, and he rose to his feet, ran towards the platform and shouted, 'I need God!' as the tears ran down his cheeks. As he fell to his knees, his face in his hands, Floyd was the first one there. He placed his big arm around his shoulders and began to call on heaven—several of the other men who were there, some of them officers in the church, gathered around as well and you never heard such a prayer meetin' in all your life!! You could hear the women's voices from different sectors of the camp crying out to God, 'Save him Jesus,' 'Deliver his soul from hell, oh Master!' Once Anna Lar had recovered and saw what was happening, she went into high gear and really began to belt it out! Gossipy old Sadie Brown looked on in admiration and said, 'They God! Charley Weaver's gettin' saved!!' They continued praying until Charley got 'prayed through' and once he began to wipe the tears away, his face was glowing like an angel. He would go on to serve the Lord faithfully for the rest of his days, and was blessed with a fine wife and a large family, all of whom went on to serve the Lord as well.

The afternoon continued on, with the news of the day being Charley Weaver's salvation. Anna Lar felt 'specially proud that it all happened while she was privileged to be singin.' One group after another sang their hearts out, and the feasting never stopped either. Where all that food seemed to come from was hard to tell—canned and picked delights, all kinds of meats and breads, pies and cakes, cookies...there was just no such thing as going to a Tarheel event of any kind and going away hungry!

Dusk had begun to fall, and the end of a wonderful day was upon them. Sassafras Walker was going to be the last to sing, and everyone always looked forward to her participation. In fact she was selected especially for the 'final touch.' 'Sassie' was a big woman—she probably weighed close to 300 pounds, and had Indian blood in her background. But she had a voice that would lift you up to heaven, and was widely known for her uninhibited praise to God. (Some said that she hadn't gotten far at all away from those Indian roots of hers!) She was a simple, no-nonsense woman, and was not impressed by anyone, nor did she try to impress anyone. She was who she was, and that by the grace of God. But you just never knew what was going to happen when Sassie got up to sing.

Things had been pretty quiet for the last couple of hours, some folks kind of worn out by all the shoutin' they'd done in the morning and early afternoon. And there was kind of peaceful feeling that dominated the camp. But...those Jones boys! They were up to somethin'! Those three little tykes already were well-known for their pranks and mischief. They weren't bad boys, but they did like to keep things 'stirred up.' They had been down by the river and in the woods all day, and that's why things had gone quite well. But now that it was getting dark, they came back to camp, and began to look around for opportunities to have some fun. They'd been to the hickory shed so many times that it didn't even matter any more—they'd even devised ways to fool their momma and daddy, to make it seem like their thrashin's were really doin' the trick. But these poor exasperated parents didn't know what else to do and every time those boys would be up to their tricks again, they'd faithfully pull out the hickory switch.

The Jones boys showed up at a very hallowed moment— Sassie was singing 'There is POWER in the Blood,' and every time she'd sing POWER, she'd open her eyes wide and look toward heaven with a great big smile on her face. The boys quickly made their plan. They had fabricated some pretty effective peashooters, and had become darn right good with 'em. In fact, Jacob just that day had felled a little sparrow, just with his peashooter. They looked at each other and grinned, and moved into place to put their plan into action.

As they surreptitiously made their way around toward the side of the platform, where they'd have a good shot, no one seemed to pay mind to them. Their folks were off starting to pack up their things, and most folks were focused on Sassie. They waited for the precise moment and when Sassie sang 'POWER' Jacob Jones fired his peashooter with all his lungs could blow, and it hit right on target—right directly on Sassie's behind! Just as she sang 'POWER' she felt this hot sting that made her jump and immediately grab the wounded area. When she did that, the elastic on her 'breeches' which had seen its last leg a long time ago, gave way, and they fell down around her ankles! Because she was right in the middle of her song, she didn't quite know what to do as she rubbed her sore behind, and contemplated leaning over and picking up her fallen breeches. But that would have been too obvious, so she just kicked them off to the side, and tried to go on with her song. Those Jones boys, not expecting such entertainment, had quickly evacuated themselves from their firing point, and showed up on the other side of the platform, while Sassie looked around for who was responsible for her dilemma. Those boys were doubled over with laughter, and several in the crowd, at first unaware of Sassie's peril, wondered what was so funny. But the news quickly made its way around, and as much as she tried to go on with singing, all eyes were more focused on her breeches than on her. When Sassie realized she'd lost her crowd, she quickly went over, picked up her breeches, stuffed them down the front of her dress, and grabbed the cane she used to walk. 'You whippersnappers, I'll done get ye yet!' and as fast as her legs could carry her, made her way off the platform and began rushing around the grounds, cane in the air, trying to figure out who it was. Those Jones boys had quickly gotten away, and most everyone knew who the culprits most likely were—but they were enjoying the spectacle too much, and tried to calm Sassie down in her fruitless pursuit. Floyd made his way up front, and couldn't help but chuckle himself—as dignified as possible. It was time to dismiss the 'sing.' 'Well folks, the good Lord has done blessed us in a mighty way today, and we need to thank Him for all his blessings. We're gonna pray now...and maybe should include a little prayer for those little varmints, for when Sassie finally catches up with 'em.' With that the whole crowd laughed, Floyd dismissed them in prayer, and even Sassie was chuckling when they said their goodbyes.

It wasn't long atall after Floyd's marked conversion, that he began to feel the 'call to preach.' He didn't wait for permission from somebody to do it, he just did! But he had the feeling that this was a high and holy calling, and struggled for a few years to really believe that God was calling him, Floyd Cook, a simple country farmer, to preach the gospel. He had had several long conversations with his Uncle Henry about it and was always thankful for his wise and patient counsel. But he took his time, doing what he knew to do' until the call became too much for him to resist. And even when his already angry parents became vehement in their opposition to his 'wastin' (his) life in religion' he pursued the prize to which he was called.

This growing awareness of an already ordained plan for his life is what pushed him in all his church activities. The Tuckaseegee Baptist Association also had their eye on this promising young man, always on the look-out for another worker for the harvest field. It was finally in April of 1898 that the presbytery called him in and interviewed Floyd about his sense of calling. He had become quite adept in the Bible and was popular as a lay preacher, or a fill-in when the regular circuit preacher got sick or was unable to make the rounds. With the laying on of hands by experienced men of God, Floyd's called into the full-time ministry was confirmed, and was another high point in his spiritual growth and development. The whole family was there for his ordination service, with Alice and their (at that time) four children sitting right in the front row. Even though it was raining and somewhat cold out, there was joy in the camp!

After the service, Floyd met with the ordination committee and was formally assigned to a circuit. The adjustments were made for others who were part of the same loop, and all rejoiced to see that the work of the Lord was moving forward and growing.

The circuit emcompassed quite a large area but it wasn't long before Preacher Floyd was known and loved far outside of Caney Fork. There was so much to do, and so little time! He now had in his charge five churches, where he would preach at each one once a month. In addition to the preaching and Bible teaching, there was the visiting—the never ending visiting that was so crucial for the extension of the gospel. He was not one to simply preach to the people and leave—he would linger and talk with different ones, and was often invited for lunch, or something to eat. He would take advantage of these spontaneous invitations to further or deepen his teaching, and address specific problems the family was having. And there was a host of those to go around! Drinking was often the cause of the rest of the problems that surfaced, but he ran into everything! Sexual mores were quite lax as well, and it was regular fare to address issues of fornication and adultery once in awhile even, involving closely related kinfolk. It took the wisdom of Solomon to address some of these issues and, for the most part, his counsel and advice were warmly and gratefully received. But there were times when that was far from being the truth, and he actually risked his life as he rode around preaching the gospel. Once in awhile he would get word of a veiled threat that would come his way, which would stiffen Alice's back with fear. But Floyd was not one to back down—no sir! Once he took a position on a certain subject, you just as well tangle with a polecat than get him to change his mind. He was bound by the Word of God and his comission by the Holy Ghost, and there warn't nobody gonna move him from there!

As his stature grew with his colleagues and fellow ministers, he was asked to serve on several different committees when the annual 'sociation' meeting came around. It was celebrated every August, and as was typical for all its members, the different committee assignments were rotated from year to year. Floyd served as co-chairman of the Foreign Missions Committee in 1902; in 1909 he was appointed to the Orphanage Committee. This committee work was especially gratifying to him, as he had such a place in his heart for the children— he just couldn't seem to get enough of "lovin' on those kids" whether they were his own, or someone else's. But he was especially moved by the condition of the orphans, who through no fault of their own, were left without a momma and daddy. Floyd chaired the committee this year and its report is as follows:

"The report on Orphanage was read by W.F. Cook for the committee. The report was ably discussed by W.F. Cook, W.H. Creasman, S.F. Woodard and W.R. Bradshaw. Report was awarded making amount to be raised $165.00. Report was adopted as follows:

Orphanage

Our Baptist Orphanage located at Thomasville has been in successful operation for 25 years. During these years it has furnished homes to thousands of unfortunate boys and girls of our State, throwing around them such safeguards and influences as only a home can give. The Orphanage at Thomasville, N.C. has been a double blessing to the Baptists of North Carolina in caring for unfortunate children and developing our people in the spirit of giving, as nothing else has done. There are now 373 children in the Orphanage. It costs $7.00 per month to keep each inmate. The increased cost of provisions has brought an additional increase in maintenance. We recommend that the churches of this Association give to the Orphanage this $165.00.

W.F. Cook, Ch'm.
I.L. Green
D.W. Middleton
The moderator appointed Rev. L.W. Hooper, E. Watson, and Martin Hoyle as Committee on Sunday Schools. Minute fund was discussed by A.C. Queen, W.B. Creasman, J.L. Owen, S.F. Woodard. Singing by the Class. Collection for Orphanage was taken amounting to $392. The hour having arrived for preaching, Rev. W.B. Creasman preached from Hebrews 2:2 and gave us a message full of gospel and spirit. Adjourned for dinner.
(Minutes of the 1909 Annual Session of the Tuckaseegee Baptist Association, On microfilm; Hunter Library, WCU, Cullowhee, NC)

One can imagine the passion with which this report was presented by Floyd on a subject that he felt strongly about. It is noteworthy that although the committee sought an offering of $165, the response of the ministers present was $392, well over double of what had been solicited. Floyd obviously made his case, and those precious orphans were the ones who benefitted from his intercession on their behalf.

It was two years later, when Floyd was appointed to the Temperance Committee that some long standing tension came to a head. Floyd had become increasingly passionate over the years for the cause of temperance. Prohibition was in its infant stages on the national level, but it was a hot topic, and Floyd had not backed down from the moonshiners, and had gone head to head with more than one of them about the corruption they brought to the community and the destruction and curse they brought to their own families as well as others. But they wouldn't listen, and these exchanges became more heated and more common, especially as Floyd would thunder from the pulpit about the damnation that awaited them for tempering with the very souls of so many of God's people. The Association had actually held off a bit from appointing Floyd to the Temperance Committee, because he was so passionate! There was some feeling that this could get out of hand, and they certainly wanted to avoid that at all costs. But the moment had come, and once his appointment was announced, Floyd was as pleased as punch. He had waited for this particular committee assignment for a long time, and wanted to use it's platform as an all out war on the moonshiners.

In their committee report that was adopted, it read as follows:

> *"Temperance is one of the most needed topics to be brought before the people of our state today. It is gaining and making very great progress. Temperance means many things that are now being indulged in by our people that should be avoided. Do we believe in temperance as we should? Do we uphold the cause as we ought to? We are admonished to be temperate in all things. If we will only discharge our duty as parents, as christians, as citizens, there would be less lawlessness and more*

christian progress, more happy homes. Our missions would be greatly increased for all objects. Much labor, time, money and talent have been spent throughout our state for prohibition. Let the good citizens see that the laws are enforced and that no whiskey man be sent to the Legislative halls. Let us beware of such candidates for office. If they get hold of the law making power, the prohibition laws will go down in North Carolina.

  A.C. Bryson
  W.F. Cook
  J.M. Watson

Floyd recognized the politics that was tied up with the issue, but be that as it may, he was not afraid to delve into where angels fear to tread. With the zeal of a crusader, his place on the Temperance Committee for that year did more to shake up Caney Fork than anything had done for a long time. Floyd took it to heart, his bound duty before God to rid the country of the moonshiners once and for all. And his sermons were often directed to just that end. He was especially hard on the 'compromisers,' or those who came to church, but who secretly supported and encouraged the liquor industry—some of them were even involved in the business end of it!! Whereas before they related openly with these liquor-making kin of theirs, they now had to be more careful—that Floyd Cook was liable to expose them right there in front of God and everybody... right in the church house! But it was getting increasingly hard for the 'compromisers' to maintain a double life.

Alice was getting worried—as much as she avoided the gossips, she heard enough of it to know that there were "rumblings in the woods" and they were directed at her zealous, God-fearing husband. One night she couldn't stand it any more and confessed, 'Floyd, I's 'fraid...that ol' moonshiner talk does set my nerves on edge. Why somes even sayin' they might lynch ye!' and with that the tears were running down her cheeks as she buried her face in his chest. 'Thar, thar momma now don't you all go and worry your perty little head over nuthin' that's not worth the time of day. People says a lot of things, 'specially when the Holy Ghost is dealing with their hearts and theys don't want to yield. We'll jus' keep prayin' like always and watch what the Lord will do in fightin' our battles.' With that he clasped her small hands in his, and prayed a long prayer, casting all their burdens onto Jesus.

It was a couple weeks later when Floyd was returning from visiting ol' Grampa Grant who was housebound, that things just didn't 'feel' right for Floyd. He'd had an uneasy feeling all day long, and now as it was getting on late in the afternoon, his uneasiness increased. Grampa Grant's place was set way back from the community, and it was a long lonely horse trail that led to his house. Floyd wasn't one to be spooked, even though the folks talked about the 'haints' that lived down this very trail. But today he couldn't deny a sense of dread and foreboding that he couldn't shake.

There they were...three of 'em. Moonshiners, ever one! He

knew each one of 'em by name, and one of 'em was a distant cousin. But by the looks on their faces, they weren't no welcomin' committee. Floyd knew he had trouble. He quickly said a prayer, and moved forward on his mount. 'Well, boys, what can I do fer ye today?' He figured he might as well get right to the point and added, 'Still chasin' that devil's business are ye?' 'Preacher!' roared the most burly one. 'We's tard a you tellin' us how to live—what to do, and what not to do. Ar bisness has been fallin' off mighty fas' and we figgers yous the one to blame. A man's gotta make an honest livin' and we figgers the Good Lord has got us livin' jus' the way we is.' And with that, the other two thugs laughed out loud. 'Seein's as how you won't learn any other way, we figgers we needs to be teachin' you a lesson.' And with that each one of them pulled out a long club and started movin' toward Floyd who was still on his horse. Floyd just stayed lookin' at each one 'em, and suddenly had a burst of compassion come over him for these 'enemies of all righteousness.' He knew it would be fruitless to reason with them—they'd been brewin' this plan for who knows how long. And they weren't gonna be satisfied no how by some more 'preacher's talk.' They were just about a yard away when all the sudden a jackrabbit jumped out of the bushes right between those three and Floyd's horse. With that sudden movement and not knowing what it was, Floyd's horse reared up on his hind legs, and it was all that Floyd could do to hold on. He jumped and pranced about, and in the process kicked all three moonshiners, who somehow had been frozen in their tracks. Floyd quickly got his horse calmed down, and was shocked by its conduct—as many years as he'd had that horse, it'd been as steady and gentle-natured as its owner. He had absolutely no explanation why something like a jackrabbit should cause his horse to become so nervous like all of a sudden. Each one of those boys was nursing their wounds—one had gotten a good clip to the jaw, another looked like his arm was broke, and the third was lying in a puddle of mud, groaning and trying to regain his breathing. 'They Lord boys, I do declare—I cain't for the life of me imagine what spooked this here horse of mine." He checked over their wounds, and estimated that the only one who really needed a doctor's care was the one with the broken arm. Not one of them was about to get anywhere near that horse of Floyd's again, at least not any time soon, and he was perplexed as to how to tranport him to the doctor. Once his kinfolk who'd been rolling in the mud was able to move around normally again, he said, 'I'll take him in the wagon,' and with that they made their way to his wagon that was close by. The other moonshiner left right away, holding his jaw, which had swelled quite a bit.

Floyd followed them all the way to the doctor's, and insisted on paying the bill. Once they were all settled, Floyd didn't quite know what to say. The moonshiner with the broken arm just said, 'I guess that God of yours knows how to watch out for ye.' Floyd smiled to himself and as they made their separate ways, he again began to bless the God of heaven. From that encounter on, it wouldn't matter how hard he would rail against the moonshiners and their trade, there was never again another shadow of threat raised against Preacher Floyd.

Beyond Wolf Mountain Series

"...I SHALL GO TO (HER) , BUT (SHE) SHALL NOT RETURN TO ME."

Chapter 8

It was the summer of 1916...a wet, sloshy disappointing and frustrating July for every farmer for the whole region. It set a record for it's high rainfall *[over 15 inches of rain for the month of July alone! National Climatic Data Center, www.ncdc.noaa.gov]* , and many were worried that their crops were going to be seriously affected. For the housewives, it meant kids underfoot, and complaining about nothing to do, longing to get out and play. Most of the boys found something to do outside of the house, but the girls stayed in and many sulked.

Floyd's first grandchild, Bonnie Isabel, *[born 27 Feb 1912, Jackson County courthouse birth registry, Sylva, NC]* was a pure delight. She was Will and 'Flar's' first child, and incorporated readily into this large and growing Cook clan. Her slightly reddish blond hair, which tended to curl under, and those sparkly, mischievious blue eyes, delighted her grampa Floyd to no end. She had his unrivalled attention for a year and a half, before her sister Clara joined the family circle, and then with every passing year there were more grandchildren added to the brood. But it wasn't much of a secret that 'that Bonnie chal' had carved a special place in her grampa's heart. He often looked for an excuse just to check on how they were doing and spend some more time bouncing Bonnie on his knee. He'd then make his way with his pastoral visits, squirrel hunting, checking to see how the crops were doing, or a hundred other things that quickly ate up his time.

Flar and Will's house was a simple structure, small and set up on a hill, back a bit up into the 'holler,' but it was adequate for their needs as a small family. Both of them knew however, that if the Lord blessed them with any more 'chillen' that they would have to find some way to 'make the barn bigger.' Sometimes when Flar would get flabbergasted by the tight quarters, she'd complain, always making sure that Will was within earshot to hear of her follies. She had to organize herself well, to keep from bumping into things, and mostly she managed, but there were times when that Scot temper would get the best of her and she'd launch into a tirade. It wouldn't last for very long though, and she would quickly remember how much she had to be thankful for. God was just so good to them, and for the life of her, she couldn't figger out why; but she was glad for His blessings.

On this particular day, Will was out in the fields, trying his best to tend to the corn that was looking a little ragged under so much rain. Flar was busy as a bee cleaning the house, washing the clothes (and worrying about how she was gonna get 'em dry), tendin to those two little busy bundles of activity, and suffering under the irritability of her latest pregnancy. She was three months along, and this time it was different from her first two— this 'chal' was a lot more active, seemed to be developing faster, and required more energy. Several of her neighbors and kinfolk had said 'this one shore tis a boy!' but Flar wasn't sure; nor did she care much at this particular moment. All she knew is that she felt a bit queasy. It was drizzly out, the house was small and these little girls were always under her feet! And it wouldn't be long now till Will came home for lunch, and she had best get with it!

That old cook stove she had came with the house—she didn't know whose it had been originally, or how long it'd been there. Those type of questions didn't matter much. It was a good stove, did well with cooking, and in the winter it would warm up the house in a hurry if they were quick to get the fire started in the mornings. She was especially glad for it that summer, because it would quickly take the damp out of the house, and provide a warm, cozy atmosphere for her to enjoy. Had it been a normal July, she'd a been griping and complaining about the intolerable heat it put out, that only added to the sun's punishing rays. But this year it was different, and for that she was glad.

The fire had been going since before Will left to work. She'd spent a good while that morning puttin a stew together and it wasn't long before those tomatoes, potatoes, corn, onions, beans and fresh skinned squirrel had blended together into a tantalizing lunch. It was getting close to suppertime so she got the coffee pot brewing—it wasn't always that they could have coffee, but Floyd had been by a couple days earlier, and left a bit of coffee that someone from the church had given him. It sure smelt good when it got to brewin!'

She thought Will was taking a little bit longer than ususal, so she decided to go and call him, so things wouldn't get cold. 'Now Bonnie, you watch Clare, and be sure to keep her out of trouble,' she exhorted. 'I'll be back quicker 'n a minute, 'cause I'm goin' to call your Daddy to lunch.' With that she turned her back, went out on to the porch and down the hill and began to yell, 'Will! Supper!' He was out quite a ways, so she had to give it her best yell—she'd gone down the hill about 500 yards and continued yelling, 'till she heard him respond, 'Yeah, I'm comin.' She took a minute to marvel at the beauty of their little acre, and cast her gaze about the misty scene before her. A slight breeze came up that chilled her, and pushed her towards her warm little haven once again.

All the sudden she heard some commotion in the house—she recognized Bonnie's screams, and little Clare's screeches immediately and bolted for the house. What she saw gripped her like ice, and she thought she was going to pass out. Bonnie's dress was on fire, and the poor chal' was running outside trying to put it out! Two-and-a-half year old Clare sat screeching on the porch, helpless to do a thing. Bonnie screamed and ran—the more she ran, the more the flames grew. 'Bonnie!' screamed Flar and ran after her, hysterical with fear and not knowing what to do...she finally caught up to her, tackled her to the ground, and as she could, threw dirt on her, and at the same time tried to pull off what was left of her dress. Bonnie was burnt bad. Will had seen from afar what was happening, and came running, out of breath; he had grabbed a bucket nearby, filled it with water from the creek-fed tank, and poured it on Bonnie, effectively putting out the fire. 'Oh my God, oh my God,' moaned Flar as they carried her into the house. She mechanically picked up Clare, and tried to calm her down, and at the same time, didn't know where she was going to get the strength to deal with this. 'Will, she's goin' be alright aint she?' she cried. Will had tears running down his cheeks and quietly mumbled, 'Don't worry momma, we'll do what we can.' He pulled off the rest of her burnt dress, and with it, came great portions of her skin that had melted together. They laid her on their bed, and while Flar handed Clare to Will (who was still screaming) she brushed the tears from her eyes and went for the butter in the spring house. Bonnie laid there moaning, crying and suffering incredibly. 'I'll go get Doc Jones,' he said. 'But Will, that's all the way into town,' Flar lamented. 'Yer right…' I'll go get Mom, she'll know what to do.' When he was assured that Flar was calmed down, and tending to Bonnie as best she could, he hitched up his horse, took Clare with him, and made a beeline for his folks' house, which thankfully wasn't too far down the road.

Before he even got there, Alice had already met him halfway, and her gray eyes were fraught with worry—she had heard the girl's screams echoing through the woods, and had made her way as fast as she could. In a flash she remembered, 'They God, Floyd's dream!'

When Floyd had gotten up that morning, as he was getting dressed and pulling on his boots, he said, 'Alice, I done had a dream.' She was already getting breakfast ready, and the kids had not woken up yet. She stopped what she was doing, stared at her beloved husband, and with a low voice asked, 'Floyd?' He went on to tell her: 'I dreamed that they 'as a bunch of folks—saw lots of folks from the church. They 'as all cryin' an' singin' and prayin'...but it twarn't in the church house.' 'They God Floyd, whattya make of it'tall?' 'Today's gonna be a bad day, momma.' With that they embraced and afterwards he took her hands and prayed,

> 'Lord Jesus, we don't know what today's a gonna hold, but we put ourselfs in your hands. We pray for our babies, and our granbabies. We pray for the church folk. Oh Lord, hear our cry! And rebuke the evil one. We jus' wanna say that we love you, and trus' you Lord. Amen.'

With her heart somewhat comforted, Alice raised her apron and dried her eyes. But she knew when Floyd 'saw' something, it was gospel—it t'was sure to come to pass. Ever since his baptism, he began to 'see' as he put it. He rapidly gained a reputation in Caney Fork, and didn't take his impressions and visions lightly. He was not a man to speak idly—when he spoke, it was because he'd thought it through a great deal. He had learned to know the ways of the Lord, knowing His mighty love, as well as his terrible fear.

So when Alice saw her palid son trembling before her, she knew the death angel had come to call—she went right with him. As they rode together back to the house, to try and tend to this very serious injured little girl, Will explained as best he could what had happened. Alice said nothing about the dream.

By the time they got there, the news had rapidly got around—the neighbor kids had seen from the hill what had happened, and had quickly told their folks. Before they knew it, there were twenty or so friends and kinfolk, all offering their help, advice and condolences for this tragedy. Several of them 'put to prayin' right there in the yard, knowing the seriousness of an accident like this.

Flar had spread butter all over Bonnie's little body *[Personal knowledge passed on to the author by Clara, Winnie and Naomi]* — this was one of the popular remedies of the day, and unfortunately, based more on myth and ignorance, than proven certainty. With this treatment, Bonnie's fate was sealed, and her life ebbed slowly away as the hours passed on.

It was several hours later when Floyd showed up at the house. Word had reached him quickly through the valley grapevine, but he had gone on his circuit visit that day, and was miles away from home by the time he finally heard the news. He rode that old nag of his as hard as he could, but she was old and tired, and he thought at several points it would have been better to run than to bother with her. Floyd's voice and face was lifted towards heaven as soon as he knew, and he cried out to God the whole length of his journey back home. It seemed like forever!

When he finally got within range, that old nag just didn't have any more to give and was already lathered with sweat after running so hard. Floyd jumped off her, and began to run for the house, seeing a large group that was gathered in front, praying and singing hymns. Will saw him coming and ran out to meet him—'Daddy, it's not good.' He tried to tell him how it happened, and all that he tried to do, but Floyd wasn't listening, nor was he slowing down. He made his way through the crowd, up the steps and Alice, when she finally saw him, grabbed and hugged him and began to cry. It was at that point, that he slowed down, and just looked, mesmerized at the scene before him. Flar's eyes were red, her face swollen and looked a mess. There were various cousins, sisters and womenfolk who were trying to do something helpful, but they all stepped back when they saw Preacher Floyd enter. Flar looked up and burst into tears once again, 'Oh Papa, what am I gonna do?' He took her into his arms and they cried together. When he was finally able to sit down beside Bonnie, he gently laid his big calloused hand gently on her forehead and with tears streaming down his cheeks, he lifted his prayer. "Jesus...Jesus...touch her now

Lord. If it be your will my God, restore this precious child to us. If ever we needed you, its now Lord. I pray for your divine and perfect will, but Lord I ask you for her life!" He stayed there for several hours, only moving so that the womenfolk could apply more butter, or try to give her some water to drink. His bold voice, broken by the shock of what was happening, could be heard praying throughout the night.

Bonnie did not get better...as the hours wore on, her breathing became labored, her burns poured out her very life liquids, and she lost consciousness. She fought on for another day accompanied by her grief stricken family, but finally expired at dawn.

Floyd hugged his son Will for a long time, not saying a word. The women folk had erupted in grief, and together their voices made an eery, other-worldly sound as it carried the final news across the valley of Caney Fork. Floyd left his grieving loved ones, and went out 'by hisself.' That was his way, and everyone knew it—no one bothered him. He made his way out into the woods...the sun was up now, and it was clear enough to see. Although had it been necessary, he could have found his way to this spot in the dark. He had been here many times before, and was his special spot for talking things out with the Lord. He even had his favorite stump that he had left, as a place to sit and meditate, but it wasn't uncommon for him to walk around, and animatedly converse with God. This morning, he had very little strength; he was dejected and confused. He felt that the very light of his life had been unfairly and unexpectedly blown out. And he he needed to talk things out.

'Now Lord, you know I've been serving you for a piece, and there's not a lot of things I understand about your ways," he began…he couldn't continue. All he could see was his little darling, one minute with her laughing, giggling struggle to get to her favorite place on his knee, and the next minute, her burned and lifeless body on the bed.

Grief as he had never known it, came from deep within and there was nothing to do but let it out. He sobbed and sobbed and sobbed, falling first of all to his knees, and then finally falling prostrate on the forest floor. 'Oh my God, what are we gonna do without her?' was his heart-felt plea.

A song that he had often sung to little Bonnie—he didn't know where it came from, or even where or how he learned it, but as clear as a bell, the words and the melody slowly sifted into his mind:

> *"My Bonnie lies over the ocean,*
> *My Bonnie lies over the sea,*
> *My Bonnie lies over the ocean,*
> *Please bring back my Bonnie to me."*

It suddenly had new, terrible meaning. Grief came to him in wave after wave:

"O blow ye winds over the ocean,
And blow ye winds over the sea,
O blow ye winds over the ocean,
And bring back my Bonnie to me."

'No Lord, I can't take this! I can't let her go.'

"Last night as I lay on my pillow,
Last night as I lay on my bed,
Last night as I lay on my pillow,
I dreamed that my Bonnie was dead."

"NO!!!" he yelled and pounded his fists in the ground. "Turn it off—I cain't hear that song! Leave me alone!" and as he screamed, all he could hear were the every day sounds of dawn in the forest.

After a couple of hours of pouring out his heart, his sadness, his anger, his loss, there slowly descended upon him an unexplainable peace. As he lay among the damp sticks, moss and dirt, he could not deny that something bigger than him was taking hold, and flooding him with a peace that passes all understanding. "Lord, it's okay. You have decided, and I have decided not to question you no more. I praise you and love you Jesus." As he lay quiet and still, one last stanza to that familiar and oft-sung song, came to him:

"The heather is blowing around me,
The blossoms of spring now appear,
The meadows with greenry surround me,

Oh Bonnie I wish you were here."
[19th century lullaby for children, written in memory of Bonnie George Campbell, acontemporary Scottish folk hero; public domain]

With that,he got up and made his way home. This old Scottish folk tune continued to resound through his mind, and he curiously found himself slowly, measuredly whistling as he walked. *"Oh Bonnie I wish you were here..."*

As he entered into the familiar entrance to his own home, he walked over to the hand-pump, pumped out a bucket of water and washed his face, and combed his hair. Alice was there waiting for him, and had his breakfast ready, a big, complete 'logger's breakfast' like only she knew how to make. Bisquits, gravy, eggs, the works. Their own four children who were still at home, watched him passionately as he made toward the house, and together they rushed out to hug him. 'It'll be alright chillen, it'll be alright,' and he smiled in sweet confidence.

The next day was the 'watch' a custom some said came over from the old country. A nice dress was selected for Bonnie (donated by one of the kinfolk) and her body was washed with camphor before being dressed. The smell was strong and permeated the whole house—you could smell it clear from the road! Friends and relatives made their way to pay their respects, and plans were made for the funeral the next day. They stayed up all night, singing and praying and when the next day came around, they all made their way to the church, with the body of poor Bonnie carried in a borrowed wagon, drawn by some fine horses that were lent by another kind relative. The gray drizzle hung like a thick blanket, providing an appropriate but despised background for the grief that was shared by the whole valley.

The somber procession arrived at the cemetery, having climbed the hill that it takes to get to Balsam Grove. The simple casket was carefully lowered off the wagon, and carried to the gravesite by two of Will's brothers and when all had assembled, it couldn't help be noticed, the beauty and glory of this mid-July morning. After so many days of rain and drizzle, this particular morning had arisen with a good solid sun. The evaporating mist rose heavenward all around them. Will and Flar walked arm in arm, carrying Clare and closely accompanied by a host of loving, supporting family members.

Floyd started off, "Ever see a day so perty in your life?" He knew what he was saying. His hopeful, almost out-of-place observation, caught some in the crowd off guard. But Floyd Cook was like that; he could say things that few other people could say and get by with. He went on to talk about the life and joy that Bonnie had brought to every one of them, and how the Lord in His wisdom had decided to leave this little flower on earth just for a short time. He had taken her to heaven to 'sweeten things up fer the rest of us' and that we just need to get on with life, even though it'll be with tears and loss. He shared a couple of memories that brought chuckles to the crowd, and even caused Flar to smile. After a sermon of about an hour, he prayed, lead the crowd in a couple of hymns, and then directed those who were responsible, to lower the casket and begin throwing in the dirt. There was quite a bit of mud, and although they tried to be as gentle as possible, they slipped and slid in the process, giving an informality that was not appropriate for the occasion. Bonnie's casket was roughly but unintentionally so, dropped into the grave with a thud. At this moment Flar began to wail, Clare began to scream and things came unglued for a time. Floyd went over and drew his daughter-in-law into his chest where she continued to cry, but slowly began to recover. Will comforted his Clare, and when she saw her momma began to calm down, she too, relaxed. *[Clare was so affected by the burning death of Bonnie, that a sense of guilt stayed with her all her life: In spite of the fact that it was Bonnie the older of the two, and Bonnie that was to take care of Clare, Clare felt a great sense of guilt and responsibility over her older sister's death. Author]*

When the burial was complete, a simple headstone was placed at the head of the grave. *[Balsam Grove Baptist Church cemetery, Caney Fork, Jackson co., NC]* Some of the men had silently left, having work that was calling them in the fields, and by the time it was over, it was mostly women folk and a few older children who were left to accompany the family back home. Life had to go on.

Floyd lingered by himself for a time over the grave of his baby. That was his way and everybody knew to just leave him. With a big sigh he walked to his waiting family, and they walked together home. Over and again in his mind he sang, "Oh Bonnie I wish you were here..." but with a great peace and a smile on his face. She was his first born grandchild, and also the first to precede him to glory.

> *"...can I bring (her) back again? I shall go to (her) , but (she) shall not return to me."*
> *II Samuel 12:23*

"IN ALL LABOUR THERE IS PROFIT..."

Chapter 9

Floyd Cook was a multi-talented man—it was actually almost by force. He wouldn't have seen it that way of course—he was just doing what he had to do to feed his family!

A minister that was fully supported by his congregation, or even his entire circuit, was almost unheard of at that time, and so it was that his family's support was produced by the sweat of his own brow. In addition to his demanding pastoral and preaching schedule, he became skilled at several different professions. His farming which was back-breaking, never-ending work, was a constant—he initially started in something he had grown up watching his daddy perform, and that was a surveyor for the county. John Cook Jr. observes:

> *"From land records and censuses we see that Hence and several of his sons...received at least 25 land*

grants from the government along with just as many deeds which they bought. It's believed they owned a good portion of the western side of the Balsam Mountains from Rocky Face near Addie, NC over to Caney Fork Creek and Balsam Grove at Rich Mountain and on to Wolf Mountain...but [he] lost most of it (1280 acres) in 1877 to back taxes of $7.88!!"

(http://freepages.genealogy.rootsweb.com/~cook/)

Being accustomed to buying and selling land, it became a natural for the Cooks to also 'measure it out.' While the family never did recover the extent of their land-holdings that had once been Hence's privilege, at least Ethan and Floyd were left with the knowledge of measurin' borders, and this was put to service for many across the county. And that knowledge together with Floyd's integrity, made a winning team. He was one of the most sought after surveyors in the county, and if there were ever a question or dispute between two parties concerning a border that was raised, Floyd was called as a witness or arbitrator, and that was the end of the discussion. If a positive answer came to 'Did Floyd Cook say it?', that was the end of the discussion. Floyd's word and sense of fairness carried its weight in gold.

And of course, you couldn't be male and live in Jackson county at the turn of the century, and not know what the logging business was all about. When there was work to do in the woods, Floyd was often found out there, sometimes for weeks at a time. An admiration for Floyd's conduct in what would have been a rough and reckless atmostphere, was related by Bud Queen:

> *"[Bud] worked in the logging camps with ...Floyd. He said that the men would sit around and play cards in the evening--except... Floyd, he sat and read his Bible."* **(Email from Doris Queen Groves, 8 February, 2001)**

To endure the taunts and gain the respect of a logging crew is no easy matter. But obviously Floyd's consistent and godly character made quite an impression on many, and were something that he carried with him whether he was in the pulpit, or swinging an axe in the woods.

His last profession that he performed came to him almost by right of inheritance, and that was postmaster. His grandpa Hence also had been postmaster; under the Confederate States of America he served the Calvins Hill post office from its creation in 1862, till its demise in 1865. Afterwards, now under the federal government at Webster which was the county seat, he was called on again serving from 1875 to his death in 1885. Floyd's uncle Jim received the same post from 1885 to 1912. Floyd himself was appointed to a new post at Cowarts (Rich Mountain) in 1910 and continued there until his death. And daughter Lorena continued her daddy's work from 1920 till that post office was closed in 1929, making the fourth generation of Cooks to serve in the postal service. Floyd fit the postmaster job like a glove—what with his outgoing personality, and his love for people, he actually saw it as an extension of his pastoral duties and took great delight in attending to the people´s needs. Often he would even bring the mail right to folks' homes, even though that was not part of his job. He would stay at the post office (which was actually housed in the General Store and Merchandise) from its regular hours, 8 AM to noon, Monday thru Friday.   And if a shut-in or widow had received something, he was sure to take it to them personally. It was this personal touch that won the hearts of his community, and put them to defend him on the rare occasion when someone would have a beef about 'Preacher Floyd.' On many occasions, he would be asked to read the letter out loud, as many of the mountain folk were illiterate, not having had the oppurtunity to 'school theyselves.' Sometimes it was good news, which would lighten the heart of a worried wife or mother; other times it would be bad news, informing of the sickness or death of a loved one far away. And on increasing occasions, there were letters from Washington territory, telling of the wonders of that beautiful place—trees so big around that five or men, touching finger to finger, would not complete the circumference!! With the promise of higher wages, and logging 'till Jesus comes back' many made their way out west, and not a few of those adventurous ones were Floyd and Alice's kinfolks.   Sometimes he would dream about travelling out west, wanting to see 'fo' hisself' if all these wonders were just 'tol' tales' or if they were really true. But with all his family here, and the good life that they had, even though it was hard, it was enough to calm any fleeting aspiration to explore any new territory.

"...AN HORROR OF GREAT DARKNESS..."

Chapter 10

Floyd had been reading his Bible since before dawn and his heart was stirred by a passage he had read many times throughout his more than 20 years in the ministry:

> *"And when the sun was going down, a deep sleep fell upon Abram; and, lo, an horror of great darkness fell upon him. And he said unto Abram, Know of a surety that thy seed shall be a stranger in a land that is not theirs, and shall serve them; and they shall afflict them four hundred years; And also that nation, whom they shall serve, will I judge: and afterward shall they come out with great substance. And thou shalt go to thy fathers in peace; thou shalt be buried in a good old age. But in the fourth generation they shall come hither again: for the iniquity of the Amorites is not yet full. And it came to pass, that, when the sun went down, and it was dark, behold a*

smoking furnace, and a burning lamp that passed
between those pieces. In the same day the LORD
made a covenant with Abram..." Gen. 15:12-18

Floyd was by now a renowned preacher—in addition to his
regular circuit, he had his pastoral duties, as well as other
invitations that would come to him from around the county,
and sometimes, even as far away as Tennessee. This
particular morning he looked back over his life, and
could've shouted as he remembered the many instances of
the grace of God, as well as His faithfulness over the years.
But having read this passage in Genesis, he was left strangely
disturbed and wondered what it was the Lord was saying to
him? He continued to ponder and meditate over it for a long
while. Finally, he was interrupted in his thoughts by Paul,
now 14 years old, who'd awakened early and wanted him to
come and help him with a young buck that was giving him
trouble. Floyd rose up and accompanied Paul to the stable,
but for the rest of the day, for the life of him couldn't get this
passage out of his mind. He knew the Lord was speaking.

It was a busy day—the never ending toil in the fields was a
regular part of his daily fare. Now that the children were
older, it wasn't so hard as it once was, but he still was out at
the crack of dawn, making sure his family was to be well
cared for. In addition, there were the regular pastoral visits he
had to make. The congregation of Balsam Grove Baptist
church had grown over the years, and there were always
needs to tend to as shepherd of the flock. There wasn't a
minute to spare in this busy man's life, but as he made his

rounds, that passage from Genesis and Abraham's experience with God, dominated his thoughts.

The day ended after supper—after he'd gathered the family to pray as was customary, he went to bed and immediately fell into a deep sleep. The family had grown...Lorena, Will, Grace, Ben and Susie had already married and had started their own families. There was less noise in the house now, but it didn't matter—Floyd had learned to concentrate, read, study, and even sleep with an active family about him. It wasn't long before he was snoring away.

The first thing he saw was the smoke...it was thick, and black, and abundant. He couldn't see where it was coming from, but the fire that produced it had a heat that could be felt but not seen. The darkness was heavy, and prevented him from gaining his bearings. This was a strange place, and Floyd was frightened. As he choked and groped away around the darkness, he suddenly found himself flying... there were sounds of laughter, of cursing; there was liquor— or was it? Men and women, lustfully falling over one another...one minute, Floyd was in the air, and another his feet touched the ground running. There were children, crying, abandoned. There was music—loud, ungodly music, and the constant, unending laughter that seemed to be mocking him. He could find no relief from the smoke...where was he? It seemed like a different place, but familiar—he recognized the voices..or did he? Why did things seem familiar, and yet so foreign? He had the sensation of betrayal, of failure, and of loud and constant mockery...what was that?

A huge idol, in the form of...what was it? There were people everywhere—he couldn't see their faces, but he could hear their voices...some were fornicating before this hideous idol, and always, always that twisted, perverse laughter. He groped his way around, tripping over someone, running into another but never quite seeing their faces. Again he was flying, far and away, but the darkness never lifted, nor did the smoke abate. 'They God,' he thought, 'I must be in hell.' Or was it the children of Israel while Moses was gone, receiving the commandments? He could make no sense of what was happening to him. Though he never stopped this flight...or run...or trip...once in awhile he would stumble on a small group, huddled together that the smoke had not seemed to touch. In fact, he heard some of the most beautiful singing he could remember—he heard prayers being offered, and tears shed...he could even hear echos of some of his own sermons, and interspersed with them, were other voices who seemed to be preaching as well. While this momentarily brought him hope and joy in this most horrid of places, it wasn't long till he was again forced into the torment from which he so longed to escape...he felt that his body was being forced through a knothole. He heard screams, and more cursing—arguing. And the incessant crying of children. Were they from an orphanage? Was this a war? The heat increased and by now he was sweating profusely...tears were streaming down his cheeks, as he sought to make sense of what had happened to him. He was now falling down a huge shaft, falling, fallling with an ever increasing speed. And suddenly, it was over. He opened his eyes, and the first thing he saw was his dear wife Alice, tenderly sleeping at his side.

His eyes focused on the familiar surrounding of their bedroom. He immediately was aware that he was wet with sweat; his cheeks were saturated with tears. It must've been a dream, he thought. How did all this happen and Alice not wake up? She must be 'tard' as a coon hound after a long hunt. He eased himself out of bed, dried himself off a bit, and went out into the kitchen. He sat at the table for the longest time in silence, going over and over in his mind of what he had seen. He knew what he needed to do, and with that made his way to a favorite part of the house where he did his prayin.' His family had been comforted through the years to either go to sleep, or often awake, to the sounds of his heart-felt intercessions before the throne of God. Even though sometimes he got somewhat loud, they had learned to sleep through it, and it was a good thing, as he had some mighty talking to God to do this night.

After he spent a good while pouring out his heart, and trying to find relief from his confusion, at long last there descended upon him that old familiar peace. He knew that God would make known to him, in His own time and way, the meaning of this dream. So he could go ahead and go back to sleep. Floyd made his way to their bedroom once again, smiled gently as he looked upon Alice's worn face, and eased into bed without her even making a move.

It was three days later, while he and Alice were in the fields hoeing, pulling weeds and working as they had done together for the past thirty some years, that Floyd began to talk. 'Alice, I done had a dream the other night, and it's right got me skeered,' he said as his voice broke. 'Floyd? What ch'all see?' He went on to tell her all about the dream, and how he could still remember it, three days later. He told her of how he'd woken up, and then went on to pray. 'Darlin,' he said, 'I's afraid that ar family's gonna leave the ways of the Lord. I don't now believe that it's ar kids we needs to be a worryin' about... but the grandkids, and their chillens. I think we's in for some hard times...probably the whole country. And I do believe that a lot of ar loved ones are gonna go their own way.' With that he was by now crying, broken hearted over the prospect of losing even one of his own kin and blood from the ways of the Lord. As they had done so many times in their married life, they dropped what they were doin' and joined hands together in prayer. First it was Alice who prayed, alarmed at the consideration that after all they had done to steer their children right, that something would happen to affect their own children and lead them down the path of destruction. She prayed for a good while, as Floyd cried his heart out. Once she finished and wiped away her own tears, Floyd by now had regained his composure and passionately prayed for the salvation and testimony of his children, and grandchildren. The sun by now had grown hot overhead, and they decided to retire to the shade of a nearby tree and eat their small lunch they'd packed.

Months went by, and with them the change of the seasons. Floyd's preaching seemed to take on an urgency that folks hadn't heard before. He often seemed preoccupied, and didn't have patience for frivolous things as he once did. There were a couple of folks in the church who had commented on his 'fresh touch' from the Holy Ghost, but most seemed not to notice. They were content to have church as always, and regardless of what the preacher said, things were always gonna be the same and they were happy with that. Floyd had a growing irritation with 'the compromisers,' those who didn't really seem to hear—their 'social tomfoolery' made him angry, and he would sometimes even say something from the pulpit. But he already knew it was in vain—unless the Spirit of God did something to change their hearts. It was fruitless to 'get on a soapbox.' He wondered if Moses had felt the same way with the children of Israel?

There were lots of changes in the family, and maybe this is what had Floyd so dadgummed fired up. His daddy had died the previous summer, having lived a long full life...he was eighty four years old. It was just five months later, in January, when his momma, greatly affected by the loss of her life-time companion, also slipped away. He missed them both but had to chuckle as he remembered her funeral— she'd always been a big woman, and when she died, they had to make a special casket just for her—nothing else would fit her! Somebody said it looked just like a piano case! And he had to admit, that's what it looked like! What would momma think to know she was buried in a 'piany case?' he chuckled—she probably would've have cursed and spat tobaccy. Oh well, stranger things had happened in Tarheel country.

Winter had turned into spring, spring into summer, summer

into fall, and now winter was knocking once again on their door. There'd been a good harvest that year, and the revival meetings were especially encouraging after a few years of a lower-than-usual attendance and spiritual apathy that several of the area ministers had lamented. Thanksgiving was a memorable celebration and time of joy—the whole family was present and the house was full. Floyd and Alice now had fourteen living grandchildren, all of them under eight years old, and the last five having been born that year! The latest arrival was Naomi Ellen, Will and Flar's newest, who had made her arrival at the end of September. So it was a beehive of laughter, babies crying and busy chatter the whole day. Floyd felt especially thankful, and he read from the Bible prior to praying for their Thanksgiving feast:

> *"Give thanks unto the LORD, call upon His name, make known his deeds among the people. Sing unto him, sing psalms unto him, talk ye of all his wondrous works. Glory ye in his holy name: let the heart of them rejoice that seek the LORD. Seek the LORD and his strength, seek his face continually. Remember his marvellous works that he hath done, his wonders, and the judgments of his mouth; O ye seed of Israel his servant, ye children of Jacob, his chosen ones. He is the LORD our God; his judgments are in all the earth. Be ye mindful always of his covenant; the word which he commanded to a thousand generations..." I Chronicles 16:8-15*

"Now chillen, we's got a lot to be thankful for to the Lord—

He's been SO good to us Cooks, especially this year. Look at all these precious babies that's crawlin' round here! We Cooks do believe in 'be fruitful and multiply!—that's one commandment we enjoys! But I wants you kids to know how much I love you, and I earnestly call upon you to serve the Lord all the days of your lives. Why the Bible says "be ye mindful always of his covenant; the word he commanded to a thousand generations." My prayer is that all of us and each one, will be 'mindful.' Don't ya'll ferget now, ya hear?" And with that small sermon finished, and the kids grabbing for food on the table, Floyd put to praying. He prayed for each one of his kids, their spouses and their children. And most of all, he thanked the Lord for all of His bounty and goodness to them, just plain ol' sinners.

With Thanksgiving behind them, and Christmas not far away, Floyd's mind was set on making it a good Christmas. They weren't much for gifts—nobody was in those days. There just wasn't any money for it. But they could do one thing good and that was eat! So Floyd determined that he was gonna get him some of the biggest and fattest squirrels he could find, and really end this year of 1920 well. It was sometimes a challenge to find squirrels during the winter, but that's what he enjoyed about the hunt. He went out a couple of times, and came back empty-handed, not unusual for this time of year, even for an excellent marksman like Floyd Cook. But he had hope that there were still some out there, and he'd keep at it, till he'd gotten what he wanted.

It was just a week before Christmas and he still hadn't

bagged those squirrels he wanted. It had gotten cold the last few days, really cold. Snow had fallen and blanketed the whole valley, and as beautiful as it was, it also brought with it a kind of depression, probably because those danged squirrels were no where to be found. But he would still go out every day, checking out different spots, hoping that they would have fresh squirrel pie for Christmas dinner. This particular day when he out, there was a rare fog that had descended on Caney Fork that made being outside all the more miserable. He figgered he'd be out for a couple hours, and if he didn't get anything, he'd just have to call it off and they'd have to settle for chicken instead of squirrel.

As he went through the woods that he knew like the back of his hand, he heard some very familiar chirping in the distance—a squirrel! Who'd a figgered on a day like this, that he'd 'a struck gold! But he stealthily made his way towards the sound, totally determined to get this elusive creature. Actually from the concert he was hearing, there was two or maybe three together!! Thank you Jesus, he breathed. He was so excited that he wasn't watching real well where he stepped, and the next step he took, was right into the icy creek! He fell chest first, and that icy water pricked him like poker's from a blacksmith's anvil. He quickly got up, and tried to shake himself somewhat dry, but couldn't stop. He just had to get those squirrels! It was about ten minutes later when he spotted them—big, fat, blue squirrels, some of the best he'd seen in a long time!! With his expert aim, he fired one after another and got all three of 'em!! Boy was he proud!! He quickly bagged 'em up, and wasn't gonna waste any time in this cold—it could freeze a man to death!

As he made his way back to the homestead, a tremendous wind came up, forming ice on his moustache, and penetrating his bones through his wet clothes. He had started to cough by the time he made it to the nearest house, which was Lorena and Terrel's, but was more concentrated on his catch than his cold. Lorena made him pull off his wet clothes and put them near the fire to dry; she gave him some of Terrel's for the meantime, while she made him some coffee and a bit to eat.As he sat and told her all about the hunt, he was interrupted several times by his coughing, which worried Lorena. She had seen enough of that in her young years, to know that it could turn deadly. She made sure that his clothes were completely dry before she let him go on home. 'Daddy, you take care of that coughin' now y'hear.' 'Don't worry your perty little head now child, you knows your momma will have me well in no time.'

But he didn't get better—even by the time he got home, his cough had turned persistent and Alice got him right into bed. She started in with her poltices, and home remedies, but Floyd's cough continued throughout the night. He wanted to get those squirrels skinned, but Alice would have none of it. She had their boys take care of it, while she tended to her sick husband.

Two days had gone by, and Floyd had not improved—the doctor had called twice, and was concerned each time he examined his patient. 'Alice, I don't like what I'm hearin' in them lungs a'his. We needs to be a'prayin.' Word got out quickly that Preacher Floyd was sick and as quick as you could bat an eye, their was family and church folks and neighbors coming by to see what they could do. Most of them brought something to eat, but Alice left it for the kids as she had no appetite to feed. And almost all of 'em put to praying that God would have mercy on this deeply loved man.

The third day the cough had transformed into a low rumbling in his lungs—he had a fever, and no matter how many blankets they had piled on him, he was chilled. Pneumonia! A word that struck terror in the hearts of Caney Fork residents—that, along with 'tuberculosis, and diphtheria' had taken so many lives through the years. There were few families who had not been touched by these 'angels of death.' Alice fought panic as she continued to tend to Floyd. Once more the doctor came and this time said, 'Alice, I've done all I can do—he's in the Lord's hands now.' She started to cry, and was comforted by her friends and family who were there for the duration.

Floyd had not lost consciousness, nor gone into deliriums—but his raspy prayers could be heard often, as he called out to the Lord. In the beginning, he prayed for restoration of his health, but as time went on and his condition deteriorated, his prayers centered on his family—Alice, his children, and those precious grandchildren that he loved so dearly.

Alice noticed a change when he asked for his boys: they had

been close by during the whole time, but came and went as their responsibilities demanded. But Floyd had called, and wanted to speak with his boys. When the last one had gotten word and arrived, a scene reminiscent of a very similar one long ago unfolded. In the Bible, in the book of Genesis as Israel lay dying, he too called in all twelve of his sons, and prophesied over them one by one. Alice was numb with grief and tried to busy herself with housework, not wanting to understand what was happening.

The first to go to his daddy's side was their youngest, Paul, who was 15. 'Stay true to your momma boy, and help her— she's gonna need you more than ever.' Paul on a grief-stricken impulse, threw himself over Floyd and hugged him, crying, but was quickly pulled away by others who were nearby. Then it was John, the sweet singer of the family, now 17. 'John boy, sing your heart out for Jesus,' was all he could muster out before a coughing spell overtook him. It took awhile for him to regain a bit of strength, and was he left as white as a ghost after that episode. Eular had been the most resistent to coming; he did not handle grief well, and was quite broken up. He almost seemed resentful and found it difficult to express his feelings. Floyd motioned for Eud to come close, and for others who were near by to leave them alone. Eud leaned his ear down right next to his daddy's mouth, and as he did so, the tears sprang from his eyes. Once that private message was passed, Eud, who was trembling uncontrollably, couldn't handle it anymore; he kissed his daddy on the cheek and turned on his heels and ran out of the house.

Next it was Ben, now 25 and already showing signs of a love for preaching. 'Son, take heed to the ministry which you have received in the Lord—fulfil it, chya' hear?' It took Ben back a bit, like his daddy was reading his mind. 'Y-y-es daddy,' he was able to blurt out, but then was left without itwords as the tears flowed down his cheeks. Finally was Will, now 30 and well established in his own family. 'Keep the banner wavin,' and again a coughing bout cut short whatever else he was going to say. Will knew immediately what his daddy was referring to, having heard this biblical phrase quoted so many times throughout his life. He'd seen it lived out in his folks' simple ways, and his heart burst at this moment in wanting to reach even half of the love they had transmitted. In other words, 'Boy, you be sure and let love be what identifies you and yours."

With every gasp of air, the color drained from his cheeks. Alice made her way to his side once again, taking his hand in hers. The folks in the rest of the house were praying and quietly singing. With one last loving look at Alice, he squeezed her hand and breathed his last. Alice through herself over him and cried till there were no tears left, her family guarding a faithful vigil around her. And so it was that Floyd Cook finished his earthtly life, and joined his loved ones around the throne of glory, never to look back.

EPILOGUE

Floyd was buried three days before Christmas, 1920 in Balsam Grove Baptist cemetery, beside the church he had pastored so faithfully off and on for fifteen years. His brother Sam Riley had this to say:

> *"Ah'd been comin' and takin' care of the cows for him. On the night Floyd died, Ah was walkin' down the road, and as Ah got even with Floyd's house, Ah heerd the most beautiful singing Ah'd ever heerd in ma life. Ah joined in and sang with "them" and knew what it meant--Floyd had died. Ah could never forget that beautiful sangin' nor that Ah done sang with them—only thang is Ah could never 'member one word a' what they sang."*

Floyd's obituary reads as follows:

> *"Rev. W.F. Cook was born August 7th, 1865 just following the war which brought such devastation and grief to our Southland. He was married to Miss Alice Parker on the 11th day of March, 1885. To their union were born eight*

children, five boys and three girls, seven of whom belong to the Baptist church.

Bro. Cook joined the Balsam Grove Baptist church October 9th, 1885 and was baptized by Rev. A.B. Henson. He was ordained to the office of deacon October 6th, 1887 and as he served in his Lord's work being led by the Holy Spirit, he was advanced to a broader field of work. He was ordained to preach the Gospel of Jesus Christ to a needy world of mankind on the 16th day of April, 1898 by a Presbytery, most of whom have fallen asleep, but whose memories are still revered.

Bro. Cook labored as a minister for twenty two years and nine months with great success, but it seemed that his last year was the most successful of any period of his ministerial life. He was ready to go and was waiting his call. He had great sympathy for all who were needy and in distress.

He was safe in counsel, either moral or spiritual and was liked and trusted by one and all. We shall miss him; but our loss is his great gain. Love, sympathy and prayers to and for all the bereaved family and friends of Bro. Cook.

He is gone but his loving memory is still with us.

Done by order of the Jackson County union Meeting in Session January 29th, 1921.

A.C. Queen
T.C. Bryson
Geo. M. Reeves
Committee

Special memorial services were also held a few months later, which were announced as follows:

"Memorial services will be held at Balsam Grove Baptist Church beginning on Friday before the second Sunday in March at 11 A.M. and continuing two services each day for three days.

Rev. Calvin Massingale the present pastor will preach on Friday at 11 A.M. and Rev. J.H. Owen at 7:30 P.M.

Brethren R.L. Cook and L.H. Crawford, A. C. Queen and others are expected to be present and take part in the memorial services.

A.C. Queen

At a special session of the Tuckaseegee Baptist Association, the following was noted:

A memorial service was held in memory of Rev. W.F. Cook, late one of the most useful pastors of this

Association. Remarks were made by Rev. A.C. Queen, R.F. Jarrett, Rev. T.F. Deitz, and Z.V. Watson.

The following resolutions were adopted:

Whereas in the year 1920 the Lord called from this m___ant** life our beloved Brother W.F. Cook to the life where sorrow, sickness and death never can mar and separations never come.

Therefore Be it Resolved: 1st: That we reommend to this Association and all who knew him his life, example and expressed in word and deed, in faith, patience, zeal and steadfastness in Christian service, as worthy to follow in Jesus Christ.

2nd, and that this Association extend its sympathy, love and prayers to the family and relatives, and more especially to those to whom he preached, who refused the message of life brought to them--their refusal and unsaved condition being the greatest burden in his dying moments; and to the world we recommend the example of his loyalty, steadfastness, love and service, measured by the gospel of Jesus Christ.

> *Signed your committee,*
> *A.C. Queen*
> *T.C. Bryson*

Z.V. Watson

The hour for preaching having arrived, Dr. A.E. Brown occupied the pulpit and preached a great sermon from the text, "Is the young man Absalom safe?" After the sermon a collection amounting to $495.00 was taken to clear off a balance due for the erection of two additional rooms to the present administrative building of the Sylva Collegiate Institute. The Association then adjourned to meet with the John's Creek Church on Thursday before the third Sunday in August, 1922.

Thus closed possibly the greatest session of the Tuckaseegee Association."

Of particular note is the last comment: **'Thus closed possibly the greatest session of the Tuckaseegee Association."** How much of that was attributed to Floyd cannot be assessed, but it was that writer's perception that the greatest session of the 'Sociation' coincided with the memorial service of Floyd Cook, a greatly loved servant of God.

Many changes took place in Floyd's family after his passing. In 1923 his oldest son Will, together with his large family, made the long train trek out to Washington state, following the lead of so many others friends and family members would have emigrated. They were the first of Floyd's family to go west, but not the last.

Shortly after Floyd's death, his daughter Lorena was appointed postmistress and continued serving in that roll at Rich Mountain. This post office was finally closed February 28. 1929. Lorena was also the first of Floyd's children to follow him home to glory, the summer of 1941.

Alice continued to serve the Lord and His church faithfully until her death in 1933. At one point at least, she was sent as a delegate to the Tuckaseegee Baptist Association Annual Meeting, in 1926.

Floyd's greatest legacy was not the many inspiring sermons he preached, nor was it the large family he fathered. It wasn't the churches he so faithfully pastored, nor the other church offices he held in the Association. It was the simple, deep and profound love that he inculcated in his children, that united them in close bonds of fellowship and friendship that were never broken. Through joy and tears, misunderstandings, tempers, and arguments, successes and failures, the banner of God's love for us, and our love for one another, was faithfully and constantly waved, to be comissioned from generation to generation. And so a faithful, simple tarheel preacher left his mark on the humble world which was Caney Fork, Jackson County. An influence that was to move even beyond the memory of Floyd's own name and relationship, as well as this little piece of God's country.

"That the generation to come might know [them,

even] the children which should be born; who should arise and declare them to their children: That they might set their hope in God, and not forget the works of God, but keep his commandments: Psalm 78:6-7

** undeciperable word in newspaper article (page 133)

MINISTERS AND
CHRISTIAN WORKERS

Out of an estimated 700 direct descendents of William Floyd Cook, the following have been identified as having served in some type of full-time ministry:

FIRST GENERATION:

REV. BEN COOK: (Ben[2], Floyd[1]) Called into the ministry in 1921 (the year following his father's premature death), he followed Floyd's footsteps. Ordained with the Southern Baptist Convention, he preached the gospel for over 50 years in western NC.

REV. EULA COOK: (Eula[2], Floyd[1]) Ordained in 1952 in his local church, he served as pastor at Hamilton Community Church in Hamilton, WA periodically in the 1950's.

SECOND GENERATION:

MARTIN COOK: (Martin[3], John[2], Floyd[1]) Founder (1964) and director of the popular Southern Gospel "Inspirations" Quartet; voted in 1972 by SGMA fans as the number one favorite gospel group in America. The Inspirations travel full-time year-round, and are well known for their 'Singin' in the Smokies' events every year in Inspiration Park, Bryson City, NC.

RUBY (COOK) HUSTON (Ruby (Cook) Huston[3], Eula[2], Floyd[1]) Remarried in 1961 as a widow with 2 little boys, Ruby joined her husband Billy Huston in the ministry and together they have pastored seven churches, from Washington state to Texas in almost 40 years of ministry. Their last church, from which they retired was First Baptist Church, Orange, TX

ZINNIE (HOOPER) WILLIS: (Zinnie (Hooper) Willis[3], Grace (Cook) Hooper[2], Floyd[1]) Zinnie's husband Clifford Willis was ordained in August, 1971 at Rock Creek Baptist Church in Bryson City, N.C. He has pastored a church for all of the 30 years except one and is presently the pastor at Flats of the Middle Creek Baptist Church in Macon County, NC. Zinnie has faithfully accompanied him and supported him in the work of the Lord for the length of their married life.

THIRD GENERATION:

MYRON COOK: (Myron[4], Martin[3], John[2], Floyd[1]) Bass player for the Inspirations

REV. CLIFF PARKER: (Cliff Parker[4], Faye (McMahan) Parker[3], Susie (Cook) McMahan[2], Floyd[1]) Called into the minstry in May 1987, Cliff has preached the gospel since June of that same year, currently pastoring New Savannah Baptist Church in Franklin, NC.

FOURTH GENERATION:

DAVID HOOPER: (David Hooper[5], Bob Hooper[4], 'Red' Ethan Hooper[3], Grace (Cook) Hooper[2], Floyd[1]) Surrendering his life to Jesus in 1996, David serves as president of Athens Bible Bookstore, Athens, GA. He is worship leader for Mt. Olive Baptist Church in Athens, GA and has a growing interest in missions, having travelled to Brazil and the Czech republic ministering the gospel.

REV. DAN JOHNSON: (Dan Johnson[5], Pauline (Pyatte) Johnson[4], Winnie (Cook) Pyatte[3], Will[2], Floyd[1]) Called into the ministry in 1976, and in full-time ministry since his graduation from NW College, Kirkland, WA in 1980, Dan was ordained with the Assemblies of God in 1983. He has pastored in WA state, served with Teen Challenge/Seattle and has been an interdenominational missionary in Guatemala since 1990, training Latinos in cross-cultural missionary service.

REV. TIMOTHY MOORE: (Timothy Moore[5], Vance Moore[4], Essie (Hooper) Moore[3], Grace (Cook) Hooper[2], Floyd[1]) Called into the ministry in 1989, he obtained his B.S. degree from Criswell Bible College and Texas, to be followed by a Masters from SW Seminary. Tim was ordained in 1991 with the Southern Baptist Convention and currently is Pastor of Evangelism and Discipleship at Woodlawn Hills Baptist Church, North Asheville, NC.

SCRIPTURE REFERENCES TO CHAPTER HEADINGS

Chapter 1   *"THIS CHILD IS SET FOR THE FALL AND RISING AGAIN OF MANY..."*
             Luke 2:34

Chapter 2   *"...A SPIRIT PASSED BEFORE MY FACE, THE HAIR OF MY FLESH STOOD UP..."*
             Job 4:15

Chapter 3   *"...A CUNNING HUNTER, A MAN OF THE FIELD..."*
             Genesis 25:27

Chapter 4   *"...IF ANY MAN BE IN CHRIST, HE IS A NEW CREATURE..."*
             II Cor. 5:17

Chapter 5   *"HE WHO FINDS A WIFE, FINDS A GOOD THING..."*
             Prov. 18:22

Chapter 6   *"...THY CHILDREN LIKE OLIVE PLANTS ROUND ABOUT THY TABLE...*

Psalm 128:3

Chapter 7   *"...HE COUNTED ME FAITHFUL, PUTTING
ME INTO THE MINISTRY."*
I Timothy 1:12

Chapter 8   *"...I SHALL GO TO (HER) , BUT (SHE)
SHALL NOT RETURN TO ME."*
II Samuel 12:23

Chapter 9   *"IN ALL   LABOUR THERE IS PROFIT..."*
Prov. 14:23

Chapter 10   *"...AN HORROR OF GREAT DARKNESS..."*
Genesis 15:12

BIBLIOGRAPHY

From Ulter to Carolina: The Migration of the Scotch Irish to Southwestern North Carolina, by H. Tyler Blethen and Curtis W. Wood Jr., Raleigh, NC Dept. of Cultural Resources, Division of Archives and History (1998)

The Civil War Reader edited by Richard B.Harwell, Mallard Press (1957)

The Highland Scots of North Carolina, 1732-1776 by Duane Meyer, Chapel Hill, University of NC Press (1957)

A History of the North Carolina Third Mounted Infantry Volunteers U.S.A.: March 1864 to August 1865 by Ron V. Killian, Heritage Books Inc. (2000)

North Carolina Troops 1861-1865: A Roster edited by Weymouth T. Jordan, Jr., North Carolina Division of Archives & History (1990)

The Scotch-Irish: A Social History by James, G, Leyburn Chapel Hill, The University of North Carolina Press (1962)

**Sketches of Western North Carolina Historical and Biographical** by Cyrus L. Hunter, Raleigh, The Raleigh News Steam Job Print (1877); reprinted by Heritage Books, Inc. (1995)_**The Trail of Tears: The Story of the American Indian Removals 1813-1855**_ by Gloria Jahoda, Wings Books, NY (1975)

Descendants of William Floyd Cook

1 William Floyd Cook b: August 07, 1865 in Jackson co., NC d: December 20, 1920 in Sylva, NC

. +Sarah Alice Parker b: Bet. September 22, 1870 - 1871 in Jackson co., NC d: September 27, 1933 in Jackson co., NC

.... 2 Lorena Isabella Cook b: January 16, 1887 in Jackson co., NC d: June 10, 1941 in Jackson co., NC

.... +Tyrrell T. Corn(e) b: July 20, 1887 in Sylva, NC d: January 25, 1969 in Sylva, NC

.... 3 Lawrence Ray Corne b: September 02, 1914 in Cowarts. Sylva, NC d: July 07, 1984 in Sedro Woolley, WA

.... +Nina Mae Queen b: September 26, 1922 d: August 04, 1990 in Sedro Woolley, WA

.... 4 Kenneth Ray Corne b: Abt. 1939

.... +Edna Hockett b: Abt. 1940

.... 5 Arlene Corne

.... 5 Michael Corne

.... 4 Jerry Edward Corne b: Abt. 1941

.... +second wife ?

.... 4 Bessie Lorena Corne b: 1943 in NC d: 1943 in NC

.... 4 Charles Henry Corne b: Abt. 1944

.... +Gail Talgenhoff

.... 3 Jessie Floyd Corn b: May 19, 1917 d: March 05, 1969

.... +Pearl Thornton

.... 4 Frances Joyce Corn

.... +Rusty Thames

.... 5 Dusty Thames

.... 4 Elizabeth Ann Corn

.... +? Langston

.... 4 Linda Jean Corn

.... +Doug Thames

.... 5 Gwen Thames

.... 5 Susan Thames

.... 5 Nancy Thames

.... 4 Barbara Sue Corn

.... 4 Jessie LaVerne Corn

.... 4 Floyd Pearson Corn

.... 3 Lilla Mae Corn b: March 1920 in WA

.... +Johnnie 'Huff' Queen b: May 30, 1916 in NC d: May 13, 1992 in Lyman, WA

.... 4 W. L. Queen b: Abt. 1941

.... +Martha Leona Gibbs b: Abt. 1943

.... 5 Brian Jason Queen b: Abt. 1967

.... 4 Doris Queen b: 1943

.... +Robert Wayne 'Bob' Groves b: Abt. 1940

.... 5 Scott Alan Groves

.... 5 Kenneth Edward Groves b: Abt. 1965

.... +Lori Eileen Jordan b: Abt. 1968

.... 6 Jordan Alan Edward Groves b: Abt. 1990
.... 6 Karina Groves b: Abt. 1993
.... 4 David Ronald Queen b: 1947
.... +June Elaine Mitchell b: Abt. 1950
.... 5 Matthew David Queen b: 1970
.... 5 Caryn Maria Queen b: Abt. 1977
.... +Rodger Funkster
.... 2 William Ethan Cook b: March 01, 1890 in Sylva, NC d: November 27, 1950 in
Everett, WA
.... +Flora Viola Aiken b: October 18, 1890 in Sylva, NC d: October 23, 1974 in
Marysville, WA
.... 3 Bonnie Isabelle Cook b: February 27, 1912 in Caney Fork, Sylva, NC d: July 12,
1916 in Caney Fork, Sylva, NC because of a stove fire
.... 3 Clara Jane Cook b: December 20, 1913 in Caney Fork, Sylva, NC
.... +Orray Snider b: October 07, 1907 d: September 1980 in Sumner, WA
.... 4 Vernon Dean Snider b: December 02, 1933 in Darrington, WA
.... +Pat Swarner
.... 5 Cheryl Snider b: August 24, 1963 in Puyallup, WA
.... +Jamie Hammond
.... 6 Kathleen Ann Hammond b: November 16, 1984
.... *2nd Husband of Cheryl Snider:
.... +Charles Gunzel b: Abt. 1959
.... 6 Luke Gunzel b: February 18, 1993
.... 6 Rachel Gunzel b: May 12, 1994
.... 6 Jacob Gunzel b: June 18, 1996
.... 5 Karen Snider b: February 22, 1965 in Puyallup, WA
.... +? Ditella
.... 6 Natasha Ditella b: March 23, 1984
.... *1st Husband of Karen Snider:
.... +Wade Mayfield b: May 17, 1963
.... 6 Taylor Mayfield b: Abt. 1996
.... *2nd Wife of Vernon Dean Snider:
.... +Dina Dayberry
.... 4 Carole Jean Snider b: May 30, 1935 in Arlington, WA
.... +Don Daniels b: May 10, 1916 d: February 10, 1989 in Olympia, WA
.... 4 Bryan Matthew Snider b: September 27, 1943 in Arlington? WA
.... +Kandi Rae Guyette b: June 16, 1946 in Seattle, WA
.... 5 Steve Snider b: June 26, 1969
.... +Sadie ? b: February 04, 1970
.... 6 Hunter Matthew Snider b: June 19, 1997
.... 5 Michael Snider b: December 22, 1971
.... 5 Bobbi Jean Snider b: February 09, 1976
.... +Kelly Hansen b: November 19, 1974
.... 6 Kaden Hansen b: April 12, 1998
.... *2nd Wife of Bryan Matthew Snider:
.... +Patti White b: Abt. 1953

.... 3 Raymond Floyd Cook b: January 10, 1917 in Caney Fork, Sylva, NC d: March 06, 1954 in Darrington, WA
.... +Elsie Marie Williams b: December 30, 1918 in WA d: August 11, 1994 in Everett, WA
.... 4 Richard Raymond 'Dick' Cook b: July 16, 1937
.... +Jeanette Elaine Paige
.... 5 Tammy Susette Cook b: Abt. 1961 in Everett, WA
.... +William Adam Badgley b: Abt. 1960
.... 6 Shawna Kristine Badgley b: December 26, 1980
.... 6 Lindsay Elaine Badgley b: September 29, 1984
.... 5 Vicki Lynn Cook b: Abt. 1963 in Everett, WA
.... +David Webb
.... 6 Tyler Charles Webb b: February 14, 1985
.... 6 Troy Raymond Webb b: October 01, 1987
.... 4 Betty Lou Cook b: January 17, 1939 in Darrington, WA
.... +Robert Kenneth Kerr, Sr. b: February 07, 1922
.... 5 Kenneth Ross Kerr b: August 10, 1959
.... +LaWonna Wilson b: Abt. 1958
.... 6 James Robert Kerr b: December 01, 1989 in Woodinville? WA
.... 6 Kathryn E. Kerr b: April 14, 1994
.... 5 Robert Kenneth Kerr, Jr. b: November 23, 1961 in Bothell, WA d: October 21, 1994 in Bothell, WA
.... +Tina ? b: Abt. 1972
.... 6 Heather Dawn Kerr b: December 17, 1986
.... 6 Tiffany Elsie Darlene Kerr b: December 30, 1987
.... 6 Michelle Louise Kerr b: April 01, 1989
.... 6 Jennifer I. Kerr b: October 13, 1990
.... 5 Anita Marie Kerr b: July 08, 1966 in Bothell, WA
.... 6 Rachel Elizabeth Kerr b: May 15, 1981
.... +Joseph Raymond Scott b: Abt. 1962
.... 6 Nicole Scott b: August 21, 1983
.... 6 Joseph Scott b: January 12, 1985
.... 6 Mishaela Scott b: May 03, 1986
.... 4 William Floyd Cook b: November 25, 1941 in Darrington, WA
.... +Nancy Hebert
.... 5 Pamela Elizabeth Cook b: December 18, 1962
.... +Dewey Ellsworth
.... 6 Kelsey Elizabeth Ellsworth b: August 26, 1989
.... 5 Terese Maria Cook b: January 13, 1964 in Everett, WA
.... +Dewey Hinricksen
.... 6 David James Hinricksen b: September 12, 1987
.... 5 Darrin John Cook b: September 25, 1966 in Everett, WA
.... +Sandy Williams b: Abt. 1968
.... 6 Child Cook b: Abt. 1990
.... 6 Child Cook b: Abt. 1995
.... *2nd Wife of William Floyd Cook:

.... +Alice Jo Raines
.... 3 Winnie Alice Cook b: August 04, 1918 in Caney Fork, Sylva, NC d: February
1994 in Everett, WA
.... +Earl Detroy Pyatte b: July 05, 1906 in Crossnore, NC d: June 01, 1966 in
Aberdeen, Grays Harbor County, Washington
.... 4 Jack Earl Pyatte b: September 24, 1937 in Darrington, WA
.... +Sue Branick b: Abt. 1937
.... 5 Dana Lorraine Davidson b: September 22, 1960
.... +Dave Nelson
.... *2nd Wife of Jack Earl Pyatte:
.... +Diane ? b: 1940 in Seattle, WA
.... 5 Tonya Rae Pyatte b: February 14, 1968
.... *3rd Wife of Jack Earl Pyatte:
.... +Yoshico ? b: Abt. 1945 in Japan
.... 5 Jackie Rae Pyatte b: May 26, 1975
.... 5 Damon Pyatte b: August 28, 1978
.... *4th Wife of Jack Earl Pyatte:
.... +Deidre Sam b: Abt. 1933
.... 4 Pauline April Pyatte b: April 01, 1939 in Darrington, WA
.... +Daniel Edward Johnson, Jr. b: April 19, 1933 in Ware, MA
.... 5 Daniel Edward Johnson IV b: June 27, 1957 in Everett, WA
.... 5 David Michael Johnson b: January 20, 1960 in Everett, WA
.... +Olene DeVille b: 1958 in Agana, GUAM
.... 6 Bianca Brooke DeVille b: March 1977
.... *1st Wife of David Michael Johnson:
.... +Judy Anette McColm b: November 22, 1958 in Tacoma, WA
.... 6 Michael David Johnson b: October 09, 1984 in Tacoma, WA
.... 6 Kelsey Marie Johnson b: April 03, 1991 in Tacoma, WA
.... 5 Sheri Lynn Johnson b: September 15, 1961 in Everett, WA d: February
04, 1987 in Soldotna, AK
.... +William Clyde Greybull b: Abt. 1960
.... 6 Tianna Marie Greybull b: January 03, 1985 in Everett, WA
.... *2nd Husband of Pauline April Pyatte:
.... +Dwayne Bailey b: Abt. 1930
.... 4 Harold Detroy Pyatte b: February 03, 1943 in Darrington, WA
.... +Shirley 'Sandy' Mills d: Abt. 1992 in Yakima, WA
.... 5 Rick Bruce Pyatte b: August 20, 1964 in Everett, WA
.... +Trish ? b: Abt. 1963
.... 6 Brandon Pyatte b: Abt. 1994
.... 6 Matthew Pyatte b: 1997
.... 5 Stacey Amber Pyatte b: November 06, 1965 in Everett, WA
.... +Brett Barbeau b: Abt. 1962 in Everett, WA
.... 6 Schyuler Pyatte Barbeau b: July 20, 1986 in Everett, WA
.... 6 Justin David Barbeau b: January 15, 1988 in Everett, WA
.... 6 Stuart Grayson Barbeau b: May 21, 1991 in Everett, WA
.... 6 Lindsay Amber-Rose Barbeau b: March 30, 1993 in Everett, WA

.... 6 Blake Daniel Barbeau b: February 24, 2000 in Everett, WA
.... *2nd Wife of Harold Detroy Pyatte:
.... +Sherry ? b: August 06
.... *2nd Husband of Winnie Alice Cook:
.... +Fred LeKey b: June 16, 1917 in MO d: December 30, 1997 in Everett, WA
.... 3 Naomi Ellen Cook b: September 24, 1920 in Caney Fork, Sylva, NC d:
            September 02, 1995 in Hoquiam, WA
.... +Charley Walker b: Abt. 1910 in NC
.... 4 Arnold Lee Walker b: July 16, 1938 in Darrington, WA
.... +Carolyn Louise Mangin b: Abt. 1940 in FL
.... 5 Jenny Walker b: May 17, 1960 in Aberdeen, WA
.... +Dave Ruler b: Abt. 1963
.... 6 Amy Ruler b: March 16, 1979
.... 6 David Ruler b: March 21, 1980
.... *2nd Husband of Jenny Walker:
.... +Alan Horning
.... 6 Alan Arnold Horning b: February 01, 1990
.... 5 Marty Walker b: November 14, 1961
.... 5 Lisa Walker b: May 01, 1964 in Aberdeen, WA
.... +Lon Tackett
.... 6 Lonzo Lee Tackett b: July 22, 1986
.... 6 Luke Martin Tackett b: August 25, 1988
.... 5 Keith Walker b: April 09, 1976
.... 4 Flora Charleen Walker Nation b: August 26, 1939 in Darrington, WA d:
            October 20, 1988 in Puyallup, WA
.... +Terry Moceri b: Abt. 1937 in Puyallup, WA
.... 5 Timothy Moceri b: December 14, 1961 in Tacoma, WA
.... +Mary Fong
.... 6 Michael Linn Moceri b: January 20, 1988
.... *1st Wife of Timothy Moceri:
.... +Michelle ? b: Abt. 1965
.... 6 Kelsey Moceri b: November 29, 1991
.... 5 Michael Moceri b: November 23, 1963 in Tacoma, WA
.... +Denise Wakefield
.... 6 Michael John Moceri b: April 1985
.... 6 Jeffery Nicholas Moceri b: July 1986
.... 5 David Moceri b: March 20, 1967 in Tacoma, WA
.... +Joelle ?
.... 6 Monica Rosa Moceri b: October 28, 1985
.... 5 Nicholas Moceri b: April 21, 1970
.... *2nd Husband of Flora Charleen Walker Nation:
.... +Dale Raught
.... 4 Peggy Diane Walker Nation b: March 01, 1941 in Darrington, WA
.... +Bruce Rowell b: Abt. 1940
.... 5 Rick Mitchell Rowell b: June 21, 1963 in Tacoma, WA
.... +Debbie Cole b: Abt. 1970

.... 6 Regan Renee Rowell b: April 16, 1989
.... 5 Rebecca Dian Rowell b: October 16, 1965
.... 5 Robert Dean Rowell b: September 14, 1969 in Tacoma, WA
.... +Wendy Nix
.... 6 Ryan Dean Rowell b: August 02, 1989 in Aberdeen, WA
.... *2nd Husband of Peggy Diane Walker Nation:
.... +Earl Ralston
.... 5 Moriah Yvonne Ralston b: May 26, 1975
.... 4 Sharon Yvonne Walker Nation b: August 30, 1942 in Darrington, WA
.... +Leslie Zehnder b: November 20, 1937 d: July 28, 1980 in Sumner, WA
.... 5 Leslie Joseph Zehnder b: September 30, 1961 in Tacoma, WA
.... +Tammy Binder b: Abt. 1963
.... 6 Kylee Anne Zehnder b: August 27, 1989
.... 5 Gregory Scott Zehnder b: January 20, 1963
.... 5 Jeffrey Alan Zehnder b: August 24, 1969 in Tacoma, WA
.... +Linda Ingham b: Abt. 1971
.... 6 Sharie Lynn Zehnder b: April 28, 1987 in Tacoma, WA
.... *2nd Husband of Sharon Yvonne Walker Nation:
.... +Jack Carlson
.... *2nd Husband of Naomi Ellen Cook:
.... +Jim Nation b: September 13, 1920 in NC d: November 24, 1990 in Hoquiam, WA
.... 4 Chuck Nation b: May 27, 1955
.... +Patsey Briden b: Abt. 1950
.... 3 Minnie Mae Cook b: July 30, 1922 in Caney Fork, Sylva, NC d: October 07, 2000 in Darrington, WA
.... +J(ohn) C(lingman) Bryson b: December 07, 1920 in Darrington, WA
.... 4 Beverly Ann Bryson b: September 17, 1941 in Darrington, WA
.... +Randy Taylor b: Abt. 1937
.... 5 John Randall "Jody" Taylor b: June 14, 1962
.... +Dorraine Holsworth b: Abt. 1965
.... 6 Jesse Bryson Taylor b: March 26, 1987
.... 6 Jacob Taylor b: 1995
.... *2nd Wife of John Randall "Jody" Taylor:
.... +Carrie ? b: Abt. 1970
.... 6 Cheyenne Taylor b: Abt. 1999
.... 5 William "Billy" Taylor b: April 06, 1965
.... +Christine ? b: Abt. 1966
.... 6 Kody Taylor b: Abt. 1993
.... 6 Kaityln Taylor b: Abt. 1996
.... 6 Dylan Taylor b: Abt. 1998
.... *2nd Husband of Beverly Ann Bryson:
.... +C.W. "Perk" Geithman, Jr. b: Abt. 1930
.... 4 Donna Arlene Bryson b: June 11, 1943 in Darrington, WA
.... +Jerry Booker b: in Darrington, WA
.... 5 Leila Mae Booker b: January 20, 1965 in Everett, WA

```
..........................  +? Hilton  b: Abt. 1955
..........................  6  Nichole Arlene Hilton Burns  b: October 17, 1985 in Everett, WA
......................  *1st Husband of Leila Mae Booker:
..........................  +Miker Davis  b: Abt. 1964
......................  6  Tyler D Allen Davis Burns  b: December 22, 1986
......................  *2nd Husband of Leila Mae Booker:
..........................  +Chance Burns
......................  5  James Dean Booker  b: August 18, 1970
......................  +Valerie Lynn Hunter  b: Abt. 1975
..........................  6  James Dean 'JD' Booker, Jr.  b: April 10, 2001
..........  3  Dolores Flora Cook  b: August 11, 1933 in Darrington, WA
..............  +Gene Butler  b: April 18, 1933 in NM  d: April 07, 1992 in Graham, WA
..............  4  Bradley Allen Butler  b: March 06, 1956 in Puyallup, WA
..................  +Julie Anne Compau  b: Abt. 1960
......................  5  Gene Allen Butler II  b: October 07, 1988 in Tacoma, WA  d: March 07,
                        1996 in Tacoma, WA
......................  5  Derrick Aaron Butler  b: August 20, 1992
..............  4  Lori Lynn Butler  b: June 10, 1963 in Yakima, WA?
..................  +Mark Wattenburger  b: Abt. 1960
......................  5  Sarah Lynn Wattenburger  b: September 14, 1984
......................  5  Daniel Curtis Wattenburger  b: January 11, 1986
..........  *2nd Husband of Dolores Flora Cook:
..............  +Carl Heidy
....  2  Grace Love Cook  b: October 14, 1893 in Sylva, NC  d: February 14, 1973 in
        Greensboro, NC
........  +Henry Bazzle "Bazz" Hooper  b: February 19, 1883 in Sylva, NC  d: May 08, 1968 in
        Cullowhee, NC
..........  3  Edgar D. Hooper  b: November 19, 1912 in Jackson co., NC  d: November 1912
        in Jackson co., NC
..........  3  Essie Geneva Hooper  b: April 01, 1914 in Brasstown community, Jackson co.,
        NC
..............  +Alvin Hooper Moore  b: September 19, 1916 in Jackson co., NC  d: July 07,
        1995 in Jackson co., NC
..............  4  Jimmy Donald Moore  b: July 07, 1934 in Jackson co., NC  d: December 18,
        1934 in Jackson co., NC
..............  4  Sandra Marlene Moore  b: August 16, 1936 in Chastain Creek, Jackson co.,
        NC
..................  +William Jenning Plemmons  b: March 30, 1934 in Haywood co., NC  d:
        January 04, 1984 in Swain co., NC
......................  5  William Michael Plemmons  b: March 30, 1955
..........................  +Sheila Howard
..............................  6  Amy Michelle Plemmons  b: March 18, 1975
......................  *2nd Wife of William Michael Plemmons:
..........................  +Marilyn 'Cookie' Gass
..............................  6  William Erick Plemmons  b: March 31, 1984
......................  *3rd Wife of William Michael Plemmons:
```

.... +Kaye ?
.... 6 William Andrew Plemmons b: August 28, 1995
.... 5 Kenneth Douglas Plemmons b: April 27, 1958 in Haywood co., NC
.... +Cheryle Wike b: December 15, 1959 in Jackson co., NC
.... 6 Megan Nicole Plemmons b: April 06, 1986
.... 6 Tanner Ryan Plemmons b: July 26, 1993
.... 5 Tony Alvin Plemmons b: August 07, 1965
.... +Laverne Wilson b: November 22, 1957
.... 4 Bessie Arlene Moore b: January 28, 1939 in Brasstown community,
Cullowhee, Jackson co., NC
.... +Glen Dexter Trantham b: May 17, 1933 in Jackson co., NC
.... 5 Sandra Arlene Trantham b: April 09, 1956 in Jackson co., NC d: Abt.
June 22, 1985 in Jackson co., NC
.... +James Buchanan b: Abt. 1954
.... 6 Kim Buchanan b: February 07, 1978
.... +Curtis Lambert
.... 6 Tyson Buchanan b: January 28, 1982
.... 5 Debra Lynn Trantham b: November 25, 1965
.... +John Buchanan
.... 6 Erick Lynn Buchanan b: February 20, 1990
.... 6 Heather Skye Buchanan b: May 06, 1997
.... *2nd Husband of Bessie Arlene Moore:
.... +Tom Barnett b: February 29, 1936
.... 4 Ora Blanche Moore b: November 04, 1941 in Brasstown community, Jackson
co., NC
.... +Jennings Yates Plemmons b: Abt. 1940
.... 5 Jeffrey Plemmons b: July 10, 1965 in Haywood co., NC
.... +Elizabeth Ross b: January 06, 1969
.... 6 Hannah Elizabeth Plemmons b: December 08, 1990
.... 6 Stephen Jennings Plemmons b: August 18, 1994
.... 5 David Jenning Plemmons b: February 14, 1968 in Murphy, Cherokee co.,
NC
.... +Karis Moody b: December 18, 1978
.... 4 Anna Frances Moore b: August 07, 1946 in Cullowhee, Jackson co., NC
.... +James Albert Awald b: February 22, 1944 in Crawford co., PA
.... 5 Randall Scott Awald b: February 07, 1967 in Asheville, NC
.... +Donna Marie Houston b: January 12, 1966 in Marietta, GA
.... 6 Anna Marie Awald b: September 30, 1996
.... 6 Patricia Ruth Awald b: February 02, 1999
.... 5 Stephen James Awald b: May 12, 1969 in Asheville, NC
.... +Wendy Beth Roles b: June 21, 1972 in Sylva, NC
.... 6 Sawyer James Awald b: February 21, 1997
.... 6 Conner Reed Awald b: March 02, 2000
.... 4 'Vance' Ray Moore b: January 12, 1949 in Jackson co., NC
.... +Carolyn Jones b: February 21, 1949
.... 5 Melody Moore b: February 02, 1968

.... +Curtis Woodall
.... 6 Slater Woodall b: July 05, 1994
.... 6 Tristan Montana Woodall b: January 1997
.... 5 Timothy Ray Moore b: June 07, 1971 in Haywood co., NC
.... +Jennifer Feichner
.... 6 Jacob Moore b: Abt. 1991
.... 6 Lydia Moore b: Abt. 1995
.... 6 Micailah Moore b: Abt. 1997
.... 4 Betty Susan 'Sue' Moore b: October 01, 1951 in Jackson co., NC
.... +Lemuel Norman b: January 1947 in Jackson co., NC
.... 5 Tammy Sue Norman b: February 27, 1976
.... +Matthew Woolard b: Abt. 1974
.... 6 Tucker Wesley Woolard b: March 28, 1997
.... 5 Crystal Ann Norman b: July 13, 1980
.... 3 Thomas Ethan 'Red' Hooper b: February 12, 1916 in Jackson co., NC d: October 28, 1977 in Sedro Woolley, WA
.... +Hazel Sitton b: Abt. 1918
.... 4 Thomas Hooper, Jr. b: July 06, 1937
.... +Carol ? b: Abt. 1940
.... 5 Tommy Hooper b: Abt. 1963
.... 5 Jerry Hooper b: Abt. 1965 d: Abt. 1981 in motorcycle accident
.... *2nd Wife of Thomas Hooper, Jr.:
.... +Marlys Tieman b: March 31, 1935 in Athol, SD d: April 13, 2001 in Bellingham, WA
.... 4 Thelma Jean Hooper b: March 07, 1939 d: May 1998
.... +Gus Hayes
.... 5 Terry Hayes
.... 5 Ronald Hayes
.... 5 Chris Hayes
.... 5 Randy Hayes
.... 4 Inavee Hooper b: April 29, 1941
.... +Kenny Cargile
.... 5 Steve Cargile b: Abt. 1960
.... 5 Wendy Cargile b: Abt. 1963
.... 5 Carla Cargile b: Abt. 1966
.... 4 Robert 'Bobby' Manuel Hooper b: February 14, 1944 in WA
.... +Linda Roweder
.... 5 Gregory Alan Hooper b: February 19, 1967 in Seattle, WA
.... +Jolie ?
.... 5 David A. Hooper b: June 17, 1971 in Seattle, WA
.... +DeMaris ? b: Abt. 1971 in GA
.... *2nd Wife of Robert 'Bobby' Manuel Hooper:
.... +Marilyn Sollid b: Abt. 1945
.... 4 Shirley Ann Hooper b: March 18, 1953 in WA
.... +David Crowell
.... 5 Carrie Crowell

.... 5 Zach Crowell
.... 3 E. Griffin Hooper b: August 10, 1918 in Jackson co., NC d: September 1919 in
          Jackson co., NC
.... 3 Sabra 'Sabrie' Hooper b: June 07, 1920 in Jackson co., NC
.... +James Lewis Goodson b: January 15, 1918
.... 4 Steve Goodson b: November 22, 1944
.... +Patricia Ann Bradburn b: November 11, 1949 d: May 04, 1989
.... 5 Melissa Ann Goodson b: 1965
.... +Albert Eastwood
.... 6 Mason Daniel Eastwood b: March 01, 1991
.... 6 Eric Hayden Eastwood b: August 07, 1993
.... *2nd Wife of Steve Goodson:
.... +Deana Moutos b: March 04, 1955
.... 3 Henry G. Hooper b: August 14, 1923 in Jackson co., NC d: January 1924 in
          Jackson co., NC
.... 3 Cyrus Jarvis Hooper b: May 03, 1925 in Jackson co., NC
.... +Freada Jo Adams
.... 4 C.J. Hooper b: Abt. 1949
.... +Lora ?
.... 5 Garrett Adam Hooper
.... *2nd Wife of C.J. Hooper:
.... +Ann Benches
.... 5 Bradley Hooper
.... 4 Gail Hooper b: Abt. 1951
.... +Ronny Parker
.... 5 Jeff Parker b: Abt. 1972 in WA d: Abt. 1985 in WA
.... 5 Steve 'Beav' Parker b: Abt. 1975 in WA
.... 4 Betty Jo Hooper b: Abt. 1955
.... +? Cloer
.... 5 Cindy Cloer
.... *2nd Husband of Betty Jo Hooper:
.... +Bill Hornbeck d: Abt. 1980 in WA
.... 5 Charles 'Chuckie' Hornbeck
.... 5 Kelly Hornbeck
.... 4 Bazzle Lynn Hooper b: Abt. 1957
.... +Inavee Trantham b: Abt. 1960
.... 5 Ashley Hooper
.... *2nd Wife of Bazzle Lynn Hooper:
.... +Jo Ann ? b: in NJ
.... 3 Agnes Magdalene Hooper b: September 06, 1927 in Jackson co., NC d: Abt.
          1998 in Swain co., NC
.... +William David Lewis b: Abt. 1925
.... 4 Judy Lewis b: Abt. 1947 d: Abt. 1947
.... 4 William Lewis b: Abt. 1949 d: Abt. 1949
.... 4 Richard David Lewis b: July 1956
.... 3 Zinnie Louise Hooper b: February 03, 1929 in Jackson co., NC

```
............. +Calvin Clifford Willis
............... 4 Bryan Jeffrey Willis  b: October 28, 1952 in NC
.................... +Georgia Grant
.................... 5 Bryan Todd Willis  b: Abt. October 25, 1972
...................... 5 Mathew Jason Willis  b: Abt. 1975
............. *2nd Wife of Bryan Jeffrey Willis:
.................... +Brenda Tishiyama  b: in Lagrange, GA
............. 4 James Lee Willis  b: October 31, 1956 in GERMANY
.................... +Elizabeth Harrington  b: in Harrisburg, PA
...................... 5 Bradley Willis  b: March 17, 1984
...................... 5 Megan Willis  b: December 23, 1989
............. 4 Gregory Preston Willis  b: January 17, 1961 in Columbus, GA
............. 4 Sherri Kay Willis  b: September 06, 1962 in Columbus, GA
...................... 5 Aleha Nicole Willis  b: June 03, 1985
......... 3 Everett Arnold Hooper  b: March 07, 1932 in Jackson co., NC
............. +Mae Dorsey
............. 4 William Henry Hooper  b: March 15, 1956 in WA
.................... +Belinda Standler
...................... 5 Brandy Hooper
...................... 5 Beau Hooper
............. *Partner of William Henry Hooper:
.................... +Janice Gage
...................... 5 Samantha Gage
............. 4 Charles Everett Hooper  b: July 09, 1957 in WA
.................... +Julie Huey
...................... 5 Calib Hooper
............. 4 Rebecca Hooper  b: November 19, 1958 in WA
.................... +Billy Self
...................... 5 Bryan Self
............. *2nd Husband of Rebecca Hooper:
.................... +Steve Johnson
...................... 5 Bristol Johnson
............. 4 Chris Hooper  b: November 16, 1967 in WA
.................... +Larry Dargitz
...................... 5 Jordan Dargitz  b: June 07, 1992
............. *2nd Husband of Chris Hooper:
.................... +Gene McNeill
...................... 5 Austin McNeill  b: November 19, 1999
......... *2nd Wife of Everett Arnold Hooper:
............. +Selah Mae Ammons
......... 3 Eudean Hooper  b: October 07, 1937 in Jackson co., NC
............. +Preston Stone Tuttle  b: October 07, 1929 in Meadows, Stokes co., NC
............. 4 Scott James Tuttle  b: March 25, 1964 in Columbus, GA
.................... +Rhonda Vinson  b: June 14, 1963
...................... 5 Jada Lea Tuttle  b: December 23, 1989 in Forest City, NC
...................... 5 Caleb Tuttle  b: March 28, 1992 in Charlotte, NC
```

.... 5 Joshua Silas Tuttle b: September 20, 1994 in Kent, WA
.... 4 Richie Dale Tuttle b: August 08, 1967
.... +Michelle ?
.... 2 Benjamin Ray Cook b: August 04, 1895 in Sylva, NC d: February 05, 1979 in Sylva, NC
.... +Pearl Leah Hooper b: May 17, 1898 in Jackson co., NC d: July 01, 1987 in Jackson co., NC
.... 3 Edgar L. Cook b: March 17, 1918 in Jackson co., NC d: February 22, 1999
.... +Mary Smathers b: Abt. 1920
.... 4 Jerry Cook b: 1947 in Waynesville, NC
.... +Cynthia Diane Grant b: Abt. 1948
.... 5 Matthew Cook b: 1973 in Knoxville, TN
.... 3 Eleanor Eunice Cook b: September 21, 1920 in Sylva, NC
.... +Horatio 'Rashio' Phillips b: August 06, 1918 in Sylva, NC d: August 09, 1985 in Sylva, NC
.... 4 Jimmy Phillips b: February 15, 1941 in Jackson co., NC d: December 1985 in Jackson co., NC
.... 4 Richard Phillips b: Abt. 1944
.... 4 Larry Dale Phillips b: Abt. 1948
.... 5 Kim Phillips
.... 5 Cynthia Phillips
.... 4 Joan Phillips b: Abt. 1950
.... +third husband ?
.... 5 Stanley ?
.... 3 Edith Cook b: March 07, 1922 in Jackson co., NC d: February 10, 1923 in Jackson co., NC
.... 3 Deith Alva Cook b: March 06, 1923
.... 3 Earl Hooper Cook b: February 09, 1925 d: February 09, 1925
.... 3 Eva Mae Cook b: April 13, 1926
.... +Alvin Rogers b: Abt. 1925
.... 4 Alan Dale Rogers b: Abt. 1946
.... 4 Linda Rogers b: Abt. 1948
.... 4 Rebecca Rogers b: Abt. 1950
.... 4 Patsey Rogers b: Abt. 1953
.... 3 Mary Helen Cook b: September 04, 1929
.... +Carroll Johnson Presley b: Abt. 1927
.... 4 Carolyn Presley b: Abt. 1950
.... +Michael Matthews
.... 5 Gabriel Matthews
.... 5 Haley Matthews
.... 4 Deborah Presley b: Abt. 1952
.... 3 J.B. Cook b: March 28, 1932 in NC
.... +Anna Laura Phillips b: 1931 in NC
.... 4 Bobby Ray Cook b: Abt. 1952
.... +Donna Gass
.... 4 Phillip Randall 'Randy' Cook b: Abt. 1956

.... +Christine Slater
.... 5 Stephen Randall Cook b: May 31, 1983
.... 5 Allison Taylor Cook b: December 09, 1985
.... 4 Susan Cook b: Abt. 1958
.... +Larry Bates
.... 5 Jonathon Edward Bates b: December 02, 1985
.... 5 Rebecca Ann Bates b: March 09, 1991
.... 3 Ruth Cook b: September 13, 1934
.... +Billy Joe Dayton b: Abt. 1932
.... 4 Michael Dayton b: Abt. 1957
.... +Pamela ?
.... 5 Rusty Dayton
.... 5 Daughter Dayton
.... 3 Ella Frances Cook b: May 09, 1940
.... +Thomas Rhodarmer b: Abt. 1938
.... 4 Ben Rhodarmer b: Abt. 1962
.... 4 Anita Rhodarmer b: Abt. 1965
.... 5 First girl Rhodarmer
.... 5 Second girl Rhodarmer
.... 5 Third girl Rhodarmer
.... 5 Fourth girl Rhodarmer
.... 4 Kelly Rhodarmer b: Abt. 1970
.... 5 Daughter Rhodarmer
.... 2 Eular Cook b: May 29, 1897 in Jackson co., NC d: January 03, 1977 in Sedro
    Woolley, WA
.... +Wilsie/Elsie Snyder b: Abt. 1901
.... 3 Daughter Cook b: Abt. 1917
.... *1st Wife of Eular Cook:
.... +Leithy A. Hoxit b: Abt. 1910 in Jackson co., NC d: October 26, 1986 in WA
.... 3 Merial Elizabeth Cook b: July 22, 1934 in Jackson co., NC d: July 23, 1934 in
    Jackson co., NC
.... 3 Ruby Cook b: February 06, 1936 in Mt. Vernon, WA
.... +Dwight Eugene Moody b: February 13, 1931 in Hamilton, WA d: October 11,
    1960 in Siskiyou, CA
.... 4 Ronnie Lee Moody b: September 03, 1952 in NC
.... 4 Don Moody b: March 16, 1957 in Bakersfield, CA
.... +Renee R. Lira b: January 15, 1964
.... 5 Olivia R. Moody b: September 29, 1991
.... 5 Hannah M. Moody b: June 09, 1993
.... 5 Caleb E. Moody b: October 10, 1997
.... *2nd Husband of Ruby Cook:
.... +Billy Edward Hutson b: July 13, 1934 in Deweyville, Newton co., TX
.... 4 Michael E. Hutson b: May 15, 1962
.... +Judy ? b: Abt. 1965
.... 5 Blake Hutson b: Abt. 1990
.... 5 Michael Hutson b: Abt. 1992

.... 5 Billy Hutson b: Abt. 1995
.... 5 Stephanie Hutson b: Abt. 2000
.... 4 Paul E. Hutson b: November 04, 1968
.... 3 Alice Cook b: September 21, 1938 in WA
.... +Claude A. Sitton b: March 19, 1933 in Caney Fork, Jackson co., NC
.... 4 David Allen Sitton b: November 19, 1955
.... +Kimberly ?
.... 5 David Allen Sitton b: September 29, 1976
.... 5 Jeremy Loren Sitton b: December 03, 1979
.... 4 Kathy Lee Sitton b: October 13, 1956
.... +? Howell
.... 5 Erin Rene Howell b: April 10, 1977
.... +Dan Cox
.... 5 Leslie Ann Howell b: October 12, 1978
.... +Ebon Brand
.... 6 Riley Austin Brand b: July 01, 1997
.... *2nd Husband of Kathy Lee Sitton:
.... +James McCartor
.... 5 Andrea Lacey McCartor b: July 12, 1982
.... 4 Daniel Ray Sitton b: June 14, 1958
.... +Georgette ?
.... 5 Kenneth Lee Sitton b: November 03, 1977
.... 6 Shiann Marie Sitton b: June 06, 1997
.... 6 Domenic Michael Austin Sitton b: December 14, 1999
.... *Partner of Daniel Ray Sitton:
.... +Jackie Shilts
.... 5 Terry Allen Sitton b: June 15, 1989
.... 5 Brandy Marie Sitton b: November 23, 1990
.... 4 Douglas Claude Sitton b: May 20, 1960
.... +Kristi ?
.... 3 Burrill Hamilton Cook b: October 20, 1939 in WA
.... +Lynn ? b: Abt. 1940
.... 4 William B. Cook b: Abt. 1961
.... 5 Billie Cook b: Abt. 1984
.... +? McCutchins
.... 6 Nathan McCutchins b: Abt. February 2001
.... 5 Nicole Cook b: Abt. 1993
.... 4 Christopher J. Cook b: Abt. 1963 d: Bef. 2000
.... 4 Laurie Cook b: Abt. 1965
.... 5 Christopher Cook
.... *2nd Wife of Burrill Hamilton Cook:
.... +Dixie ? b: Abt. 1945
.... 4 Kenneth Cook b: Abt. 1969
.... 4 Kimberly Cook b: Abt. 1969
.... 5 Son Cook b: Abt. 1983
.... 4 Shelly Cook b: Abt. 1972

```
..................... 5  Child Cook
..................... 5  Child Cook
.......... *3rd Wife of Burrill Hamilton Cook:
.............. +Vivian ?  b: Abt. 1942
................. 4  James B. Cook  b: Abt. 1975
..................... +Julia ?
..................... 5  Jacob Cook  b: Abt. 1997
................ *2nd Wife of James B. Cook:
..................... +Lisa ?  b: Abt. 1975
..................... 5  Randy Cook  b: Abt. 1994
..................... 5  Joshua Cook  b: Abt. 2000
.......... *4th Wife of Burrill Hamilton Cook:
.............. +Mari ?  b: in Japan
.......... 3  Alfred Cook  b: Abt. 1942 in WA  d: Abt. 1943 in WA
.......... 3  William A. 'Billy' Cook  b: June 18, 1944 in WA
................ 4  Son Cook
................ 4  SonII Cook
................ 4  Daughter Cook  d: 1995 in Sedro Woolley, WA
..................... 5  Child Cook
.... 2  Susan Jane Cook  b: July 01, 1901 in Sylva, NC  d: February 01, 1991 in Sylva, NC
........ +William Lawrence McMahan  b: March 15, 1895 in Jackson co., NC  d: November
           01, 1978 in Sylva, NC
.......... 3  Horace Ray McMahan  b: April 21, 1920 in Sylva, NC  d: October 22, 1988 in
           Sylva, NC
.............. +Gertie Sitton
.......... *2nd Wife of Horace Ray McMahan:
.............. +Ethel May Sitton  b: June 01, 1924  d: March 31, 1998
................ 4  James Monroe McMahan  b: July 02, 1942 in Jackson co., NC  d: December
           26, 1965
..................... +Mary Skipper  b: January 20, 1943
..................... 5  Virgil Ray McMahan  b: October 30, 1965  d: September 27, 1997
................ 4  Linda Ann McMahan  b: August 07, 1946
..................... +Joseph Medlin  b: October 12, 1940
..................... 5  James Douglas Medlin  b: April 17, 1966
........................... +Renee Adams  b: May 21, 1963
........................... 6  Joshua Lance Medlin  b: November 04, 1985
..................... 5  Sandy Allen Medlin  b: October 12, 1968
........................... +Jena Griffin  b: October 28, 1976
........................... 6  Hawk Donovan Medlin  b: September 17, 1998
..................... 5  Randy Scott Medlin  b: October 12, 1968
........................... +Lisa Hendrix  b: October 02, 1967
........................... 6  Shana Nicole Medlin  b: June 27, 1988
........................... 6  Amber Sha Medlin  b: August 03, 1991
................ 4  Phyllis Ray McMahan  b: May 04, 1951
..................... +David Ratenski  b: August 20, 1947
..................... 5  Shawn Ian Ratenski  b: January 27, 1975
```

.... +Susan Waldrop b: September 13, 1973
.... 6 Sean Michael Ratenski b: February 23, 1996
.... 4 Fred J. McMahan b: December 05, 1953
.... +Debra Jessup b: Abt. 1955
.... 5 Deanna Kay McMahan Lancaster b: March 23, 1973
.... +Kevin Day
.... 5 Jeremy Scott McMahan Lancaster b: November 05, 1975
.... *2nd Wife of Fred J. McMahan:
.... +Dana Claire Stewart
.... 5 Joshua Adam McMahan b: September 28, 1981
.... *3rd Wife of Fred J. McMahan:
.... +Betsy Anette Arrington
.... 4 Rita K. McMahan b: July 30, 1956
.... +Keith Fant
.... 5 Amanda Lee Fant b: January 23, 1976
.... 5 Ashley Kay Fant b: March 15, 1980
.... *2nd Husband of Rita K. McMahan:
.... +Bruce Dewart
.... 5 David Ryan Dewart b: November 13, 1988
.... 3 Faye Alice McMahan b: September 20, 1921 d: December 26, 1968
.... +William Harry Parker b: January 13, 1920 d: April 18, 1994 in Sylva, NC
.... 4 Olean Parker b: March 07, 1941 d: March 07, 1983
.... +Millard Gates
.... 5 Jackie Randall Gates b: September 18, 1957
.... +Gala Sue Wheatley
.... 6 Chastity Michelle Gates b: January 08, 1977
.... *2nd Wife of Jackie Randall Gates:
.... +Carol Cochran b: September 02, 1961
.... 6 Jared Randall Gates b: February 10, 1989
.... 5 Donna Lou Gates b: January 02, 1961
.... +Raymond Ray Smith b: February 19, 1958
.... 6 Joshua Dale Smith b: January 19, 1983
.... 6 Tiffany Olean Smith b: September 03, 1985
.... 5 Tamara Jean Gates b: March 18, 1963
.... +William Lee Allen
.... 6 Justin Parker Allen b: April 20, 1985
.... *2nd Husband of Tamara Jean Gates:
.... +Dennis James Ledbetter
.... 6 Nikki Lamell Ledbetter b: February 01, 1988
.... 6 Sara Lashell Ledbetter b: April 04, 1990
.... 6 Trenton Levi Ledbetter b: August 03, 1992
.... 5 Michael Dean Gates b: November 15, 1967
.... +Donna Hunt
.... 6 Shawn Michael Gates b: April 03, 1997
.... *2nd Husband of Olean Parker:
.... +Kenneth Dale Crawford b: Abt. 1938

.... 4 Clifford Dean Parker, Sr. b: January 25, 1943
.... +Glenda Faye Brown b: July 04, 1946
.... 5 Christy Faye Parker b: March 30, 1970
.... +Christopher Shook
.... 5 Clifford Dean 'Deano' Parker, Jr. b: December 12, 1970
.... +Amanda Clement
.... 6 Lauren Elexis Parker b: July 05, 1993
.... 6 Allison McKenzie Parker b: February 09, 1999
.... 5 Misty Dawn Parker b: May 13, 1977
.... +Gabriel Southards
.... 4 Bertie Mae Parker b: November 23, 1945 d: May 04, 1978
.... +Johnny Harold Moore
.... 5 Brandon Joseph 'Jody' Moore b: February 29, 1972
.... +Miranda Jo Holder
.... 6 Jonathon Tyler Moore b: April 03, 1997
.... 4 Mary Sue Parker b: January 30, 1948
.... +Willie Junior Williamson b: October 03, 1945
.... 5 Travis Scott Williamson b: June 01, 1971
.... +Sheryl Denise Howell b: June 04, 1972
.... 6 Parker Howell Williamson b: January 20, 1999
.... 3 Mattie Mae McMahan b: November 01, 1925 in Jackson co., NC
.... +Major Hooper b: February 25, 1921 in Jackson co., NC d: April 20, 1995 in
Jackson co., NC
.... 4 Virginia Hooper b: September 30, 1942
.... +Everett Bynum Mathis b: September 10, 1939
.... 5 Regina Gail Mathis b: January 20, 1965
.... +Bobby Burns b: July 23, 1961
.... 6 Trevor Justin Burns b: October 07, 1984
.... 4 Donald Carroll Hooper b: August 28, 1944
.... +Cathy Hughes b: July 21, 1951
.... 5 Jennifer Denene Hooper b: August 16, 1976
.... +Todd Stephens
.... 5 Brandon Carroll Hooper b: November 11, 1983
.... 4 Frank Eugene Hooper b: February 27, 1949
.... +Elizabeth Diane Seay b: March 14, 1954
.... 5 Christopher Brian Hooper b: May 16, 1972
.... +Janelle Watson b: August 27, 1974
.... 6 Lane Madison Hooper b: April 10, 1998
.... 5 Tracey Eugene Hooper b: August 14, 1976
.... 4 Glen Edward Hooper b: January 31, 1955
.... +Rhonda Jenkins b: March 09, 1959
.... 5 Cody Glenn Hooper b: September 27, 1991
.... 3 Bee Claude 'Blackie' McMahan b: April 23, 1928 in Jackson co., NC d: January
17, 1973 in FL
.... +Rosa V. Loftis b: November 23, 1931 d: 1992
.... 4 Brenda Faye McMahan b: June 04, 1951

.... 5 Timothy Eugene McMahan b: June 03, 1971 d: 1997
.... 6 Elizabeth Rosa Grubb b: May 15, 1994
.... 6 Cody Lee McMahan b: May 30, 1997
.... +William Ray Eagle, Sr. b: July 17, 1935 d: 1995
.... 5 Tracey Renee Eagle b: November 26, 1973
.... +William Frederick Sanders b: November 18, 1969
.... 6 Megan Nicole Sanders b: February 03, 1992
.... 5 Williarm Ray Eagle, Jr. b: July 22, 1986
.... 4 Carolyn Sue 'Connie' McMahan b: August 06, 1953
.... +Joseph Paul Thompson b: June 08, 1946
.... 5 Gina Helen Thompson b: July 09, 1974
.... 5 Eric Wayne Thompson b: August 18, 1984
.... 4 Rickey Claude McMahan b: April 03, 1958 d: April 15, 1997
.... 4 Stephen Roy McMahan b: July 04, 1961
.... +Susie Diane Miller b: November 05, 1957
.... 5 Crystal Sue McMahan b: June 05, 1979
.... +Dennis James Cox b: August 20, 1975
.... 6 Chance Brandon Cox b: May 10, 1995
.... 6 Dylan Stephen Cox b: December 10, 1998
.... *2nd Wife of Stephen Roy McMahan:
.... +Sara Beth Renegar b: April 21, 1964
.... 4 James Jeffrey McMahan b: February 14, 1966
.... +Kimberly Ann Hawks b: July 17, 1965
.... 5 James Joshua McMahan b: February 28, 1991
.... 5 Savanna Brooke McMahan b: February 28, 1991
.... 3 Dee Lloyd 'Red' McMahan b: April 23, 1928 in Jackson co., NC d: July 22, 1974
in WA
.... +Blanche Arleen Parker b: February 27, 1933
.... 4 Richard Dale McMahan b: January 08, 1950
.... +Lisa Westfall b: Abt. 1952
.... 5 William Michael McMahan b: May 04, 1972 d: April 26, 1993
.... *2nd Wife of Richard Dale McMahan:
.... +Heone Sook Kim b: August 10, 1947
.... 4 Cathy McMahan b: February 24, 1952
.... +Larry Hall b: June 23, 1950
.... 5 Tina Renee Hall b: February 05, 1970
.... 6 Larry Lee Hall b: July 29, 1994
.... 6 Preston Lee Hall b: November 06, 1995
.... 5 Rusell Dean Hall b: February 12, 1972
.... 4 Dee Allen McMahan b: August 01, 1954
.... 4 Stanley Carl McMahan b: September 23, 1956
.... +Cheryl Lee b: December 07, 1958
.... 5 Jessie Dee McMahan b: October 22, 1990
.... 3 Betty Lee McMahan b: December 10, 1930 in Jackson co., NC
.... +Keith Dale Hill b: September 12, 1925
.... 4 Lila Sue Hill b: August 06, 1947

.... +James Garland Vickers b: March 04, 1942
.... 5 Barry Dwayne Vickers b: February 28, 1964
.... +Janine Lynna Giffin b: February 18, 1968
.... 6 Stephanie Lynna Vickers b: February 09, 1992
.... 6 Katie Marie Vickers b: August 18, 1994
.... 5 Melinda Hope Vickers b: November 26, 1972
.... +Kenneth Doug Lollis b: April 20, 1970
.... 4 Margaret Ann Hill b: December 23, 1950
.... +Julian Milton Crowe
.... 5 Kimberly Denise Crowe b: February 10, 1967
.... +Jerry Leroy Merck
.... 6 Randall Garrett Merck b: October 02, 1986
.... 6 Jerry Andrew Merck b: July 06, 1988
.... *2nd Husband of Kimberly Denise Crowe:
.... +Bradley Fuller Gilreath
.... 5 Jeremy Keith Crowe b: December 22, 1972
.... +Kimberly Hope Baker
.... 6 Branson Keith Crowe b: October 22, 1997
.... *2nd Husband of Margaret Ann Hill:
.... +Stuart Barnes b: July 19, 1947
.... 3 Roy Franklin McMahan b: Abt. 1931 in Jackson co., NC d: May 21, 1957
.... 3 L. C. McMahan b: August 22, 1933 in Jackson co., NC
.... +Peggy Ann Blanton b: August 08, 1934
.... 4 Patricia Ann McMahan b: May 04, 1955
.... +Johnny Michael Cunningham
.... 5 Michael Derrick Cunningham b: March 27, 1975
.... 5 Anna Nicole Cunningham b: February 07, 1983
.... *2nd Husband of Patricia Ann McMahan:
.... +Michael Stuart Sluder b: July 14, 1952
.... 4 Terry Lynn McMahan b: April 26, 1961
.... +Dwayne Calvin Ward
.... 5 Joshua Calvin Ward b: January 15, 1983
.... 5 Tamayra Lynn Ward b: May 18, 1988
.... 4 Angela Gwen McMahan b: July 27, 1966
.... +Jackie Lee West b: January 08, 1957
.... 5 Jessica Nicole West b: December 01, 1994
.... 3 Arilla McMahan b: June 03, 1935 in Jackson co., NC
.... +Arnold Edwin Jones b: June 26, 1932 in Jackson co., NC
.... 4 Deborah Jane Jones b: December 28, 1955
.... +Alfred Lee Watson b: February 01, 1953
.... 5 Connie 'Michelle' Watson b: September 10, 1974
.... +Allen Shane Ballew b: November 07, 1973
.... 6 Clayton Allen Ballew b: February 25, 1996
.... 6 Lindsay Paige Ballew b: February 11, 2000
.... 5 Travis Dale Watson b: May 16, 1976 d: June 02, 1978
.... 4 David Arnold Jones b: June 11, 1961

.... +Tracey Cheryl Stamey b: August 28, 1960
.... 5 Russell David Jones b: February 19, 1985
.... 3 Troy Allen McMahan b: February 26, 1938 in Jackson co., NC
.... +Shelba Jean Ray b: June 26, 1939
.... 4 Pamela Jean McMahan b: April 16, 1960
.... +William Lee Hyatt b: August 01, 1959
.... 5 Jennifer Brooke Hyatt b: July 20, 1985
.... 5 Jamie Lee Hyatt b: April 30, 1991
.... 4 Cynthia Denise McMahan b: February 28, 1962
.... +Bailey Michael Ensley b: June 09, 1957
.... 5 Leann Denise Ensley b: June 01, 1985
.... 5 Logan Allen Ensley b: December 20, 1989
.... 4 Lisa Kaye McMahan b: October 23, 1965
.... +Michael Patrick Coggins
.... 5 Ashley Rae Coggins b: August 02, 1988
.... *2nd Husband of Lisa Kaye McMahan:
.... +Donald Lee Green b: October 10, 1957
.... 4 Rebecca Dawn McMahan b: February 08, 1969
.... +Matthew James Hunter b: April 02, 1968
.... 5 Emily Dawn Hunter b: January 11, 1986
.... 5 Dillon Hunter Hunter b: September 23, 1992
.... 3 (Mary) Alice McMahan b: March 15, 1941 in Jackson co., NC
.... +Harold Ensley b: Abt. 1932
.... 4 Daniel Carroll Ensley b: June 12, 1958
.... +Phyllis Arleen Cogdill b: November 30, 1957
.... 5 Joseph Aaron Ensley b: March 26, 1983
.... 5 Sarai Elizabeth Ensley b: March 24, 1981
.... *2nd Wife of Daniel Carroll Ensley:
.... +Janice Conner b: February 12, 1959
.... 4 Charles Eric Ensley b: March 11, 1966
.... *2nd Husband of (Mary) Alice McMahan:
.... +Reed Hayes Henson b: October 10, 1946
.... 4 Susan Loree Henson b: January 18, 1979
.... 2 John Lewis Cook b: May 10, 1903 in Sylva, NC d: December 20, 1967 in Sylva, NC
.... +Ellen Watson b: May 12, 1907 in Sylva, NC d: August 09, 1991 in Sylva, NC
.... 3 Arbie Cook b: 1930
.... +Woodfin Rhodes
.... 4 Judy Rhodes
.... 5 Child Rhodes
.... 5 Child Rhodes
.... 5 Child Rhodes
.... 3 Canler Cook b: 1933
.... 3 Martin Cook b: June 29, 1936 in Caney Fork, Sylva, NC
.... +Ora Blanche Shular b: Abt. 1944 in Caney Fork, Sylva, NC
.... 4 Myron Cook b: July 11, 1963
.... 4 Marsha Cook b: 1966

.... 4 Michael Cook b: May 28, 1968
.... 2 Paul Lafayette Cook b: September 23, 1905 in Sylva, NC d: May 30, 1966 in
          Concrete, WA
.... +Gennie M. Morgan b: Abt. 1910 in Jackson co., NC d: Aft. 1938
.... 3 Herman Cook b: Abt. 1925 d: Aft. June 1970
.... 3 William Floyd Cook b: Abt. 1927 d: 1955
.... +Mary ?
.... 4 Linda Cook b: Abt. 1948
.... 4 [1] Franklin Paul Cook b: August 22, 1950 in Burlington, WA
.... +[2] Patircia Lynn Hyler b: July 25, 1956
.... 5 [3] Franklin Paul Cook b: March 11, 1979 in Bellingham, WA
.... 5 [4] Christine Marie Cook b: December 27, 1970
.... 4 Carolyn Cook b: Abt. 1954
.... 3 Baxter Cook b: November 08, 1928 in Cowarts, NC d: June 14, 1970 in Sedro
          Woolley, WA
.... +Glaydelle Mathis b: January 04, 1929 in Jackson co., NC
.... 4 Gennie Cecilia Cook b: August 04, 1956
.... +Timothy Christman Petersen
.... 5 Kyle Christman Petersen b: April 27, 1983
.... 5 Kody Connor Petersen b: March 13, 1987
.... 4 Timothy Cook b: June 26, 1959
.... 3 James Arthur 'Art' Cook b: May 21, 1930 in Sylva, NC
.... +Mabel Anne Marie Campbell b: Abt. 1933
.... 4 [1] Franklin Paul Cook b: August 22, 1950 in Burlington, WA
.... +[2] Patircia Lynn Hyler b: July 25, 1956
.... 5 [3] Franklin Paul Cook b: March 11, 1979 in Bellingham, WA
.... 5 [4] Christine Marie Cook b: December 27, 1970
.... 4 James Arthur 'Jim' Cook b: October 19, 1955 in Sedro Woolley, WA
.... +Terry Payne
.... 5 Jordan Lennea Cook b: October 24, 1992
.... 4 Jeffrey Scott Cook b: March 04, 1957 in Sedro Woolley, WA d: July 06,
          2000 in Sedro Woolley, WA
.... 4 Sherry Ann Cook b: November 22, 1959
.... +Jay Lincoln Black b: July 13, 1951
.... 4 Alesia Lorraine Cook b: January 02, 1962
.... +Ronnie Dean Van Pelt b: January 26, 1962
.... 5 Dylan James Van Pelt b: March 01, 1994 in Bellingham, WA
.... 3 Marie Cook b: Abt. 1932
.... +? Pressnell b: Abt. 1930
.... 3 Allen Blaine Cook b: 1932 d: January 15, 1964 in Seattle, WA
.... +Lois Queen b: Abt. 1934
.... 4 Colleen Kay Cook b: Abt. 1954
.... +Bob Wiseman
.... 5 April Blaine Wiseman
.... 4 Joyce Aline Cook b: Abt. 1956
.... +John Lee Skelton

.... 5 Blaisha Leeann Skelton
.... 5 Holly Christine Skelton
.... 5 Kayla Justin Skelton
.... 4 Juanita Jane Cook b: Abt. 1958
.... +Ron Clark
.... 5 Keisha Marie Clark
.... 5 Keigen Blaine Clark
.... *2nd Husband of Juanita Jane Cook:
.... +Gordon Stanley Brevick, Jr.
.... 4 Carla Ann Cook b: Abt. 1960
.... +Cecil Paul Orr
.... 5 Alina Marie Orr
.... *2nd Husband of Carla Ann Cook:
.... +Phillips Hickey
.... 3 Magdalene Cook b: Abt. 1937
.... +? Hughley
.... 3 Mack Guilford Cook b: February 06, 1938 in Sylva, NC d: May 10, 1938 in
         Sylva, NC
..... *2nd Wife of Paul Lafayette Cook:
.... +Otha Shelton Parker b: Abt. 1918
.... 3 Lyle Cook b: Abt. 1959

Keep the Banner Wavin'

Ancestors of William Floyd Cook

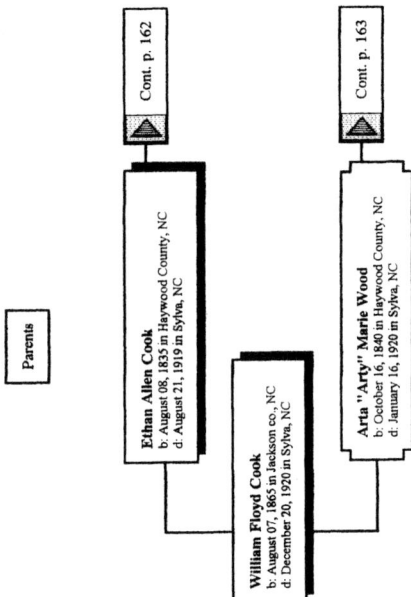

Parents

Ethan Allen Cook
b: August 08, 1835 in Haywood County, NC
d: August 21, 1919 in Sylva, NC

Cont. p. 162

William Floyd Cook
b: August 07, 1865 in Jackson co., NC
d: December 20, 1920 in Sylva, NC

Arta "Arty" Marie Wood
b: October 16, 1840 in Haywood County, NC
d: January 16, 1920 in Sylva, NC

Cont. p. 163

William Floyd Cook's ancestry is tentative,
though fairly well documented

161

Ancestors of William Floyd Cook

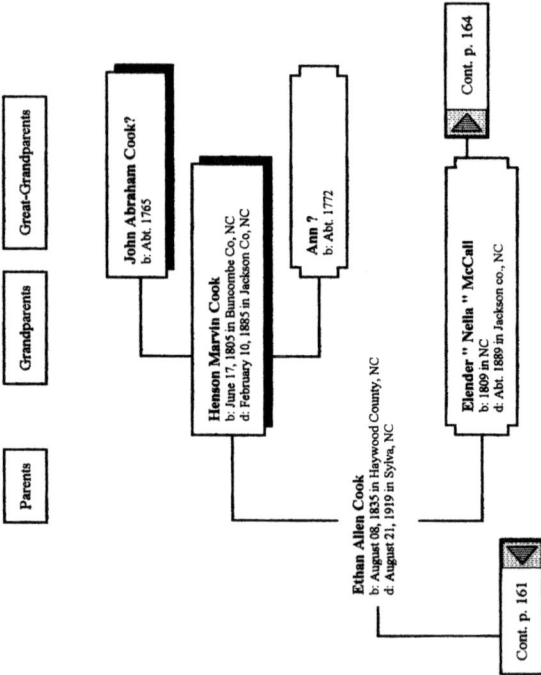

Parents

Grandparents

Great-Grandparents

John Abraham Cook?
b: Abt. 1765

Henson Marvin Cook
b: June 17, 1805 in Buncombe Co, NC
d: February 10, 1885 in Jackson Co, NC

Ann ?
b: Abt. 1772

Ethan Allen Cook
b: August 08, 1835 in Haywood County, NC
d: August 21, 1919 in Sylva, NC

Cont. p. 161

Elender " Nella " McCall
b: 1809 in NC
d: Abt. 1889 in Jackson co., NC

Cont. p. 164

Ancestors of William Floyd Cook

Parents

Grandparents

Great-Grandparents

Arta "Arty" Marie Wood
b: October 16, 1840 in Haywood County, NC
d: January 16, 1920 in Sylva, NC

Cont. p. 161

James Bryson Wood
b: Abt. 1821 in Haywood co., NC
d: Aft. June 06, 1880 in Jackson co., NC

Henry Wood
b: Abt. 1767 in Scotts Creek, Old Buncombe co., NC
d: Abt. 1840 in Haywood co., NC

Cont. p. 166

Margaret "Peggy" Bryson
b: April 11, 1784 in Ninety Six district, SC
d: January 16, 1847 in Haywood co., NC

Cont. p. 167

Eleanor "Nellie" Phillips
b: Abt. 1816 in SC
d: December 01, 1895 in Jackson co., NC

Cont. p. 165

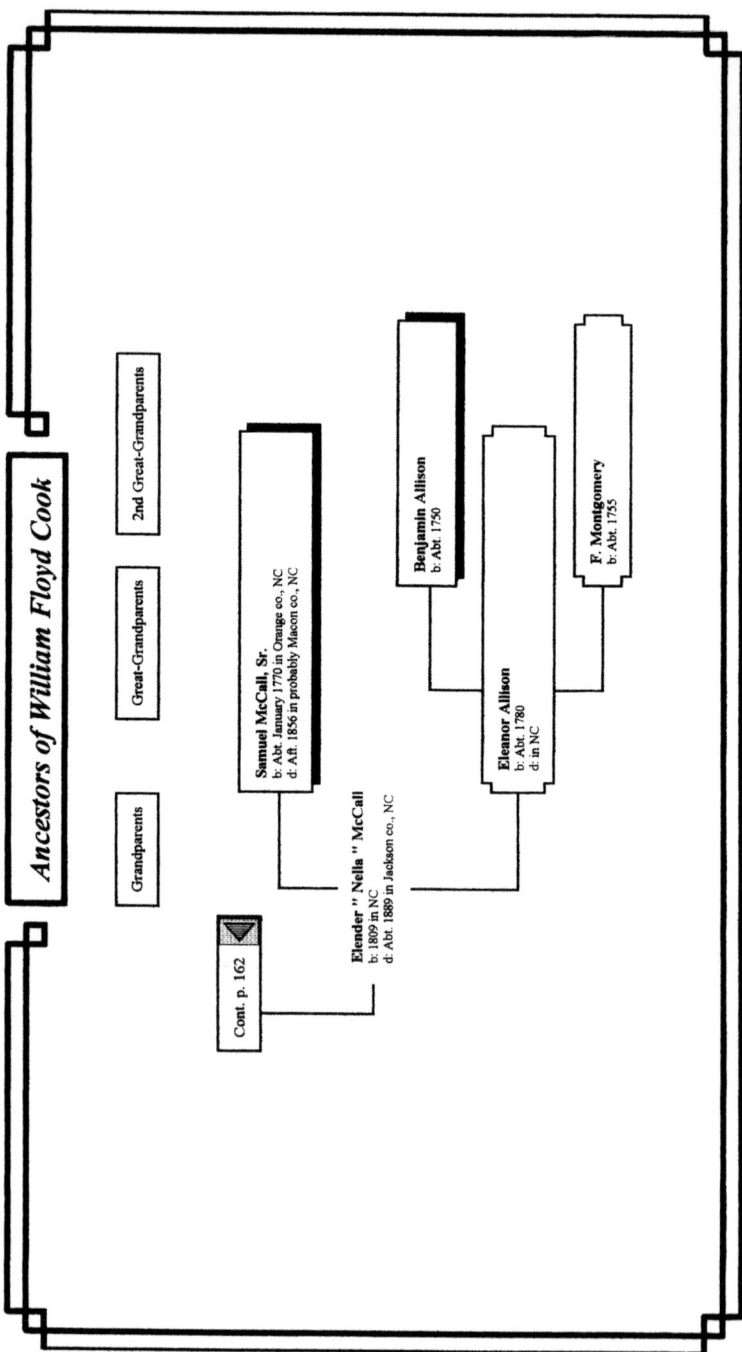

Ancestors of William Floyd Cook

Grandparents	Great-Grandparents	2nd Great-Grandparents

Samuel McCall, Sr.
b: Abt. January 1770 in Orange co., NC
d: Aft. 1856 in probably Macon co., NC

Elender " Nella " McCall
b: 1809 in NC
d: Abt. 1889 in Jackson co., NC

Cont. p. 162

Benjamin Allison
b: Abt. 1750

Eleanor Allison
b: Abt. 1780
d: in NC

F. Montgomery
b: Abt. 1755

Ancestors of William Floyd Cook

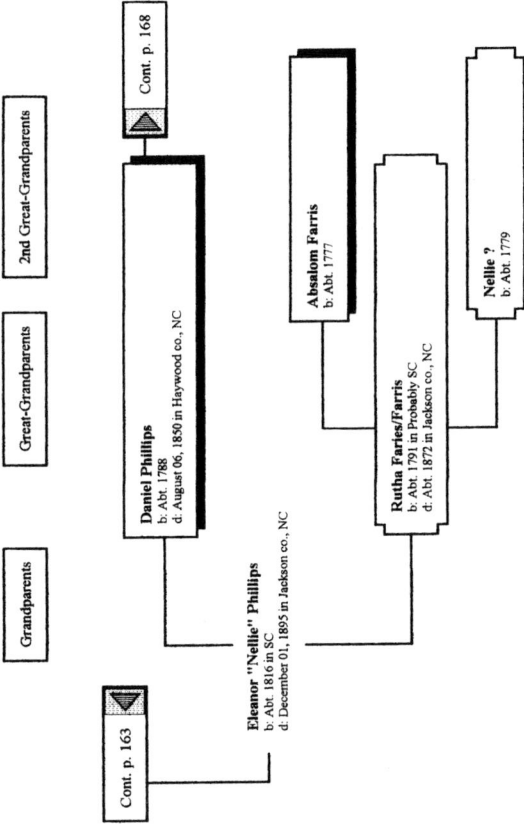

| Grandparents | Great-Grandparents | 2nd Great-Grandparents |

Cont. p. 163

Eleanor "Nellie" Phillips
b: Abt. 1816 in SC
d: December 01, 1895 in Jackson co., NC

Daniel Phillips
b: Abt. 1788
d: August 06, 1850 in Haywood co., NC

Cont. p. 168

Rutha Faries/Farris
b: Abt. 1791 in Probably SC
d: Abt. 1872 in Jackson co., NC

Absalom Farris
b: Abt. 1777

Nellie ?
b: Abt. 1779

Keep the Banner Wavin'

166

Ancestors of William Floyd Cook

Great-Grandparents

2nd Great-Grandparents

3rd Great-Grandparents

John Wood
b. Abt. 1720

James? George? Wood
b. Abt. 1750 in Scotland?
d: in TN?

Mary ?
b. Abt. 1725

Henry Wood
b. Abt. 1767 in Scotts Creek, Old Buncombe co., NC
d. Abt. 1840 in Haywood co., NC

Margaret ?

Cont. p. 163

Ancestors of William Floyd Cook

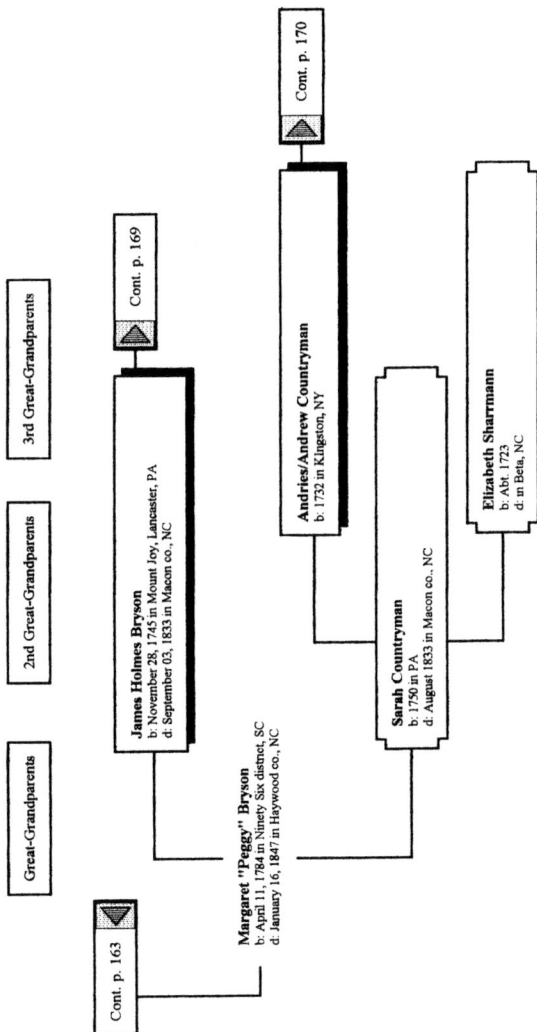

| Great-Grandparents | 2nd Great-Grandparents | 3rd Great-Grandparents |

Cont. p. 163

James Holmes Bryson
b: November 28, 1745 in Mount Joy, Lancaster, PA
d: September 03, 1833 in Macon co., NC

Cont. p. 169

Margaret "Peggy" Bryson
b: April 11, 1784 in Ninety Six district, SC
d: January 16, 1847 in Haywood co., NC

Andries/Andrew Countryman
b: 1732 in Kingston, NY

Cont. p. 170

Sarah Countryman
b: 1750 in PA
d: August 1833 in Macon co., NC

Elizabeth Sharrmann
b: Abt. 1723
d: in Beta, NC

Keep the Banner Wavin'

168

Ancestors of William Floyd Cook

Great-Grandparents

2nd Great-Grandparents

Andrew Peter Phillips
b: Abt. 1752

Sarah ?
b: Abt. 1754

Daniel Phillips
b: Abt. 1788
d: August 06, 1850 in Haywood co., NC

Cont. p. 165

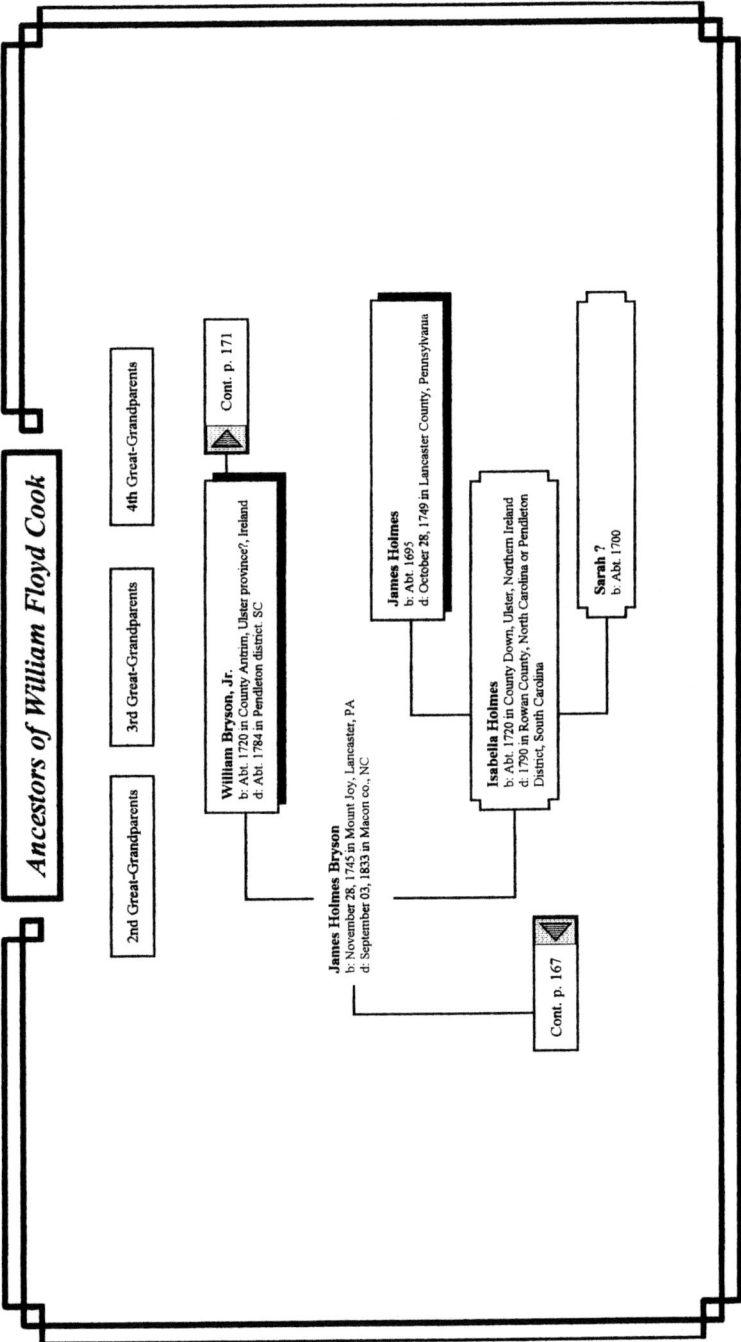

Ancestors of William Floyd Cook

2nd Great-Grandparents   3rd Great-Grandparents   4th Great-Grandparents

Cont. p. 171

William Bryson, Jr.
b: Abt. 1720 in County Antrim, Ulster province?, Ireland
d: Abt. 1784 in Pendleton district. SC

James Holmes
b: Abt. 1695
d: October 28, 1749 in Lancaster County, Pennsylvania

Isabella Holmes
b: Abt. 1720 in County Down, Ulster, Northern Ireland
d: 1790 in Rowan County, North Carolina or Pendleton
District, South Carolina

Sarah ?
b: Abt. 1700

James Holmes Bryson
b: November 28, 1745 in Mount Joy, Lancaster, PA
d: September 03, 1833 in Macon co., NC

Cont. p. 167

Ancestors of William Floyd Cook

| 3rd Great-Grandparents | 4th Great-Grandparents | 5th Great-Grandparents |

Johan Friedrich Lantzman
b: Abt. 1675

Andries Fritz Countryman/Lantzman
b: Abt. 1700

Andries/Andrew Countryman
b: 1732 in Kingston, NY

Cont. p. 167

Ancestors of William Floyd Cook

3rd Great-Grandparents

4th Great-Grandparents

William Bryson, Sr.
b: Abt. 1695

Elizabeth Byers?
b: Abt. 1700

William Bryson, Jr.
b: Abt. 1720 in County Antrim, Ulster province?, Ireland
d: Abt. 1784 in Pendleton district, SC

Cont. p. 169

Index of Individuals

?

? -

Ann: 162
Carol: 147
Carrie: 144
Christine: 144
DeMaris: 147
Diane: 142
Dixie: 152
Georgette: 152
Jo Ann: 148
Joelle: 143
Jolie: 147
Judy: 151
Julia: 153
Kaye: 146
Kimberly: 152
Kristi: 152
Lisa: 153
Lora: 148
Lynn: 152
Margaret: 166
Mari: 153
Mary: 159
Mary: 166
Michelle: 150
Michelle: 143
Nellie: 165
Pamela: 151
Sadie: 140
Sarah: 169
Sarah: 168
second wife: 139
Sherry: 143
Stanley: 150
third husband: 150
Tina: 141
Trish: 142
Vivian: 153
Yoshico: 142

A

Adams -

Freada Jo: 148
Renee: 153
Aiken -
Flora Viola: 140
Allen -
Justin Parker: 154
William Lee: 154
Allison -
Benjamin: 164
Eleanor: 164
Ammons -
Selah Mae: 149
Arrington -
Betsy Anette: 154
Awald -
Anna Marie: 146
Conner Reed: 146
James Albert: 146
Patricia Ruth: 146
Randall Scott: 146
Sawyer James: 146
Stephen James: 146

B

Badgley -
Lindsay Elaine: 141
Shawna Kristine: 141
William Adam: 141
Bailey -
Dwayne: 142
Baker -
Kimberly Hope: 157
Ballew -
Allen Shane: 157
Clayton Allen: 157
Lindsay Paige: 157
Barbeau -
Blake Daniel: 143
Brett: 142
Justin David: 142
Lindsay Amber-Rose: 142
Schyuler Pyatte: 142

Stuart Grayson: 142
Barnes -
   Stuart: 157
Barnett -
   Tom: 146
Bates -
   Jonathon Edward: 151
   Larry: 151
   Rebecca Ann: 151
Benches -
   Ann: 148
Binder -
   Tammy: 144
Black -
   Jay Lincoln: 159
Blanton -
   Peggy Ann: 157
Booker -
   James Dean: 145
   James Dean 'JD' , Jr.: 145
   Jerry: 144
   Leila Mae: 144, 145
Bradburn -
   Patricia Ann: 148
Brand -
   Ebon: 152
   Riley Austin: 152
Branick -
   Sue: 142
Brevick -
   Gordon Stanley , Jr.: 160
Briden -
   Patsey: 144
Brown -
   Glenda Faye: 155
Bryson -
   Beverly Ann: 144
   Donna Arlene: 144
   J(ohn) C(lingman): 144
   James Holmes: 167
   Margaret "Peggy": 163
   William , Jr.: 169
   William , Sr.: 171
Buchanan -

Erick Lynn: 146
Heather Skye: 146
James: 146
John: 146
Kim: 146
Tyson: 146
Burns -
   Bobby: 155
   Chance: 145
   Nichole Arlene Hilton: 145
   Trevor Justin: 155
   Tyler D Allen Davis: 145
Butler -
   Bradley Allen: 145
   Derrick Aaron: 145
   Gene: 145
   Gene Allen II: 145
   Lori Lynn: 145
Byers? -
   Elizabeth: 171

C

Campbell -
   Mabel Anne Marie: 159
Cargile -
   Carla: 147
   Kenny: 147
   Steve: 147
   Wendy: 147
Carlson -
   Jack: 144
Clark -
   Keigen Blaine: 160
   Keisha Marie: 160
   Ron: 160
Clement -
   Amanda: 155
Cloer -
   ?: 148
   Cindy: 148
Cochran -
   Carol: 154
Cogdill -
   Phyllis Arleen: 158
Coggins -
   Ashley Rae: 158

Michael Patrick: 158

Cole -
Debbie: 143

Compau -
Julie Anne: 145

Conner -
Janice: 158

Cook -
Alesia Lorraine: 159
Alfred: 153
Alice: 152
Allen Blaine: 159
Allison Taylor: 151
Arbie: 158
Baxter: 159
Benjamin Ray: 150
Betty Lou: 141
Billie: 152
Bobby Ray: 150
Bonnie Isabelle: 140
Burrill Hamilton: 152, 153
Canler: 158
Carla Ann: 160
Carolyn: 159
Child: 153
Child: 153
Child: 153
Child: 141
Child: 141
Christine Marie: 159
Christopher: 152
Christopher J.: 152
Clara Jane: 140
Colleen Kay: 159
Darrin John: 141
Daughter: 153
Daughter: 151
Deith Alva: 150
Dolores Flora: 145
Earl Hooper: 150
Edgar L.: 150
Edith: 150
Eleanor Eunice: 150
Ella Frances: 151
Ethan Allen: 161
Eular: 151
Eva Mae: 150
Franklin Paul: 159

Franklin Paul: 159
Gennie Cecilia: 159
Grace Love: 145
Henson Marvin: 162
Herman: 159
J.B.: 150
Jacob: 153
James Arthur 'Art': 159
James Arthur 'Jim': 159
James B.: 153
Jeffrey Scott: 159
Jerry: 150
John Lewis: 158
Jordan Lennea: 159
Joshua: 153
Joyce Aline: 159
Juanita Jane: 160
Kenneth: 152
Kimberly: 152
Laurie: 152
Linda: 159
Lorena Isabella: 139
Lyle: 160
Mack Guilford: 160
Magdalene: 160
Marie: 159
Marsha: 158
Martin: 158
Mary Helen: 150
Matthew: 150
Merial Elizabeth: 151
Michael: 159
Minnie Mae: 144
Myron: 158
Naomi Ellen: 143, 144
Nicole: 152
Pamela Elizabeth: 141
Paul Lafayette: 159, 160
Phillip Randall 'Randy': 150
Randy: 153
Raymond Floyd: 141
Richard Raymond 'Dick': 141
Ruby: 151
Ruth: 151
Shelly: 152
Sherry Ann: 159
Son: 153
Son: 152

SonII: 153
Stephen Randall: 151
Susan: 151
Susan Jane: 153
Tammy Susette: 141
Terese Maria: 141
Timothy: 159
Vicki Lynn: 141
William A. 'Billy': 153
William B.: 152
William Ethan: 140
Rev. William Floyd: 139, 161
William Floyd: 159
William Floyd: 141
Winnie Alice: 142, 143
Cook? -
John Abraham: 162
Corn(e) -
Tyrrell T.: 139
Corn -
Barbara Sue: 139
Elizabeth Ann: 139
Floyd Pearson: 139
Frances Joyce: 139
Jessie Floyd: 139
Jessie LaVerne: 139
Lilla Mae: 139
Linda Jean: 139
Corne -
Arlene: 139
Bessie Lorena: 139
Charles Henry: 139
Jerry Edward: 139
Kenneth Ray: 139
Lawrence Ray: 139
Michael: 139
Countryman -
Andries/Andrew: 167
Sarah: 167
Countryman/Lantzman -
Andries Fritz: 170
Cox -
Chance Brandon: 156
Dan: 152
Dennis James: 156
Dylan Stephen: 156
Crawford -

Kenneth Dale: 154
Crowe -
Branson Keith: 157
Jeremy Keith: 157
Julian Milton: 157
Kimberly Denise: 157
Crowell -
Carrie: 147
David: 147
Zach: 148
Cunningham -
Anna Nicole: 157
Johnny Michael: 157
Michael Derrick: 157

D

Daniels -
Don: 140
Dargitz -
Jordan: 149
Larry: 149
Davidson -
Dana Lorraine: 142
Davis -
Miker: 145
Day -
Kevin: 154
Dayberry -
Dina: 140
Dayton -
Billy Joe: 151
Daughter: 151
Michael: 151
Rusty: 151
DeVille -
Bianca Brooke: 142
Olene: 142
Dewart -
Bruce: 154
David Ryan: 154
Ditella -
?: 140
Natasha: 140
Dorsey -
Mae: 149

E

Eagle -
 Tracey Renee: 156
 William Ray , Sr.: 156
 Williarm Ray , Jr.: 156
Eastwood -
 Albert: 148
 Eric Hayden: 148
 Mason Daniel: 148
Ellsworth -
 Dewey: 141
 Kelsey Elizabeth: 141
Ensley -
 Bailey Michael: 158
 Charles Eric: 158
 Daniel Carroll: 158
 Harold: 158
 Joseph Aaron: 158
 Leann Denise: 158
 Logan Allen: 158
 Sarai Elizabeth: 158

F

Fant -
 Amanda Lee: 154
 Ashley Kay: 154
 Keith: 154
Faries/Farris -
 Rutha: 165
Farris -
 Absalom: 165
Feichner -
 Jennifer: 147
Fong -
 Mary: 143
Funkster -
 Rodger: 140

G

Gage -
 Janice: 149
 Samantha: 149
Gass -

Donna: 150
 Marilyn 'Cookie': 145
Gates -
 Chastity Michelle: 154
 Donna Lou: 154
 Jackie Randall: 154
 Jared Randall: 154
 Michael Dean: 154
 Millard: 154
 Shawn Michael: 154
 Tamara Jean: 154
Geithman -
 C.W. "Perk" , Jr.: 144
Gibbs -
 Martha Leona: 139
Giffin -
 Janine Lynna: 157
Gilreath -
 Bradley Fuller: 157
Goodson -
 James Lewis: 148
 Melissa Ann: 148
 Steve: 148
Grant -
 Cynthia Diane: 150
 Georgia: 149
Green -
 Donald Lee: 158
Greybull -
 Tianna Marie: 142
 William Clyde: 142
Griffin -
 Jena: 153
Groves -
 Jordan Alan Edward: 140
 Karina: 140
 Kenneth Edward: 139
 Robert Wayne 'Bob': 139
 Scott Alan: 139
Grubb -
 Elizabeth Rosa: 156
Gunzel -
 Charles: 140
 Jacob: 140
 Luke: 140
 Rachel: 140
Guyette -

Kandi Rae: 140

H

Hall -
  Larry: 156
  Larry Lee: 156
  Preston Lee: 156
  Rusell Dean: 156
  Tina Renee: 156
Hammond -
  Jamie: 140
  Kathleen Ann: 140
Hansen -
  Kaden: 140
  Kelly: 140
Harrington -
  Elizabeth: 149
Hawks -
  Kimberly Ann: 156
Hayes -
  Chris: 147
  Gus: 147
  Randy: 147
  Ronald: 147
  Terry: 147
Hebert -
  Nancy: 141
Heidy -
  Carl: 145
Hendrix -
  Lisa: 153
Henson -
  Reed Hayes: 158
  Susan Loree: 158
Hickey -
  Phillips: 160
Hill -
  Keith Dale: 156
  Lila Sue: 156
  Margaret Ann: 157
Hilton -
  ?: 145
Hinricksen -
  David James: 141
  Dewey: 141

Hockett -
  Edna: 139
Holder -
  Miranda Jo: 155
Holmes -
  Isabella: 169
  James: 169
Holsworth -
  Dorraine: 144
Hooper -
  Agnes Magdalene: 148
  Ashley: 148
  Bazzle Lynn: 148
  Beau: 149
  Betty Jo: 148
  Bradley: 148
  Brandon Carroll: 155
  Brandy: 149
  C.J.: 148
  Calib: 149
  Charles Everett: 149
  Chris: 149
  Christopher Brian: 155
  Cody Glenn: 155
  Cyrus Jarvis: 148
  David A.: 147
  Donald Carroll: 155
  E. Griffin: 148
  Edgar D.: 145
  Essie Geneva: 145
  Eudean: 149
  Everett Arnold: 149
  Frank Eugene: 155
  Gail: 148
  Garrett Adam: 148
  Glen Edward: 155
  Gregory Alan: 147
  Henry Bazzle "Bazz": 145
  Henry G.: 148
  Inavee: 147
  Jennifer Denene: 155
  Jerry: 147
  Lane Madison: 155
  Major: 155
  Pearl Leah: 150
  Rebecca: 149
  Robert 'Bobby' Manuel: 147
  Sabra 'Sabrie': 148

Shirley Ann: 147
Thelma Jean: 147
Thomas Ethan 'Red': 147
Thomas , Jr.: 147
Tommy: 147
Tracey Eugene: 155
Virginia: 155
William Henry: 149
Zinnie Louise: 148

Hornbeck -
Bill: 148
Charles 'Chuckie': 148
Kelly: 148

Horning -
Alan: 143
Alan Arnold: 143

Houston -
Donna Marie: 146

Howard -
Sheila: 145

Howell -
?: 152
Erin Rene: 152
Leslie Ann: 152
Sheryl Denise: 155

Hoxit -
Leithy A.: 151

Huey -
Julie: 149

Hughes -
Cathy: 155

Hughley -
?: 160

Hunt -
Donna: 154

Hunter -
Dillon Hunter: 158
Emily Dawn: 158
Matthew James: 158
Valerie Lynn: 145

Hutson -
Billy: 152
Rev. Billy Edward: 151
Blake: 151
Michael: 151
Michael E.: 151
Paul E.: 152

Stephanie: 152

Hyatt -
Jamie Lee: 158
Jennifer Brooke: 158
William Lee: 158

Hyler -
Patircia Lynn: 159

I

Ingham -
Linda: 144

J

Jenkins -
Rhonda: 155

Jessup -
Debra: 154

Johnson -
Bristol: 149
Rev. Daniel Edward IV: 142
Daniel Edward , Jr.: 142
David Michael: 142
Kelsey Marie: 142
Michael David: 142
Sheri Lynn: 142
Steve: 149

Jones -
Arnold Edwin: 157
Carolyn: 146
David Arnold: 157
Deborah Jane: 157
Russell David: 158

Jordan -
Lori Eileen: 139

K

Kerr -
Anita Marie: 141
Heather Dawn: 141
James Robert: 141
Jennifer I.: 141
Kathryn E.: 141
Kenneth Ross: 141
Michelle Louise: 141

Rachel Elizabeth: 141
Robert Kenneth , Jr.: 141
Robert Kenneth , Sr.: 141
Tiffany Elsie Darlene: 141
Kim -
Heone Sook: 156

L

Lambert -
Curtis: 146
Lancaster -
Deanna Kay McMahan: 154
Jeremy Scott McMahan: 154
Langston -
?: 139
Lantzman -
Johan Friedrich: 170
Ledbetter -
Dennis James: 154
Nikki Lamell: 154
Sara Lashell: 154
Trenton Levi: 154
Lee -
Cheryl: 156
LeKey -
Fred: 143
Lewis -
Judy: 148
Richard David: 148
William: 148
William David: 148
Lira -
Renee R.: 151
Loftis -
Rosa V.: 155
Lollis -
Kenneth Doug: 157

M

Mangin -
Carolyn Louise: 143
Mathis -
Everett Bynum: 155
Glaydelle: 159
Regina Gail: 155

Matthews -
Gabriel: 150
Haley: 150
Michael: 150
Mayfield -
Taylor: 140
Wade: 140
McCall -
Elender " Nella ": 162
Samuel , Sr.: 164
McCartor -
Andrea Lacey: 152
James: 152
McColm -
Judy Anette: 142
McCutchins -
?: 152
Nathan: 152
McMahan -
(Mary) Alice: 158
Angela Gwen: 157
Arilla: 157
Bee Claude 'Blackie': 155
Betty Lee: 156
Brenda Faye: 155
Carolyn Sue 'Connie': 156
Cathy: 156
Cody Lee: 156
Crystal Sue: 156
Cynthia Denise: 158
Dee Allen: 156
Dee Lloyd 'Red': 156
Faye Alice: 154
Fred J.: 154
Horace Ray: 153
James Jeffrey: 156
James Joshua: 156
James Monroe: 153
Jessie Dee: 156
Joshua Adam: 154
L. C.: 157
Linda Ann: 153
Lisa Kaye: 158
Mattie Mae: 155
Pamela Jean: 158
Patricia Ann: 157
Phyllis Ray: 153

Rebecca Dawn: 158
Richard Dale: 156
Rickey Claude: 156
Rita K.: 154
Roy Franklin: 157
Savanna Brooke: 156
Stanley Carl: 156
Stephen Roy: 156
Terry Lynn: 157
Timothy Eugene: 156
Troy Allen: 158
Virgil Ray: 153
William Lawrence: 153
William Michael: 156

McNeill -
Austin: 149
Gene: 149

Medlin -
Amber Sha: 153
Hawk Donovan: 153
James Douglas: 153
Joseph: 153
Joshua Lance: 153
Randy Scott: 153
Sandy Allen: 153
Shana Nicole: 153

Merck -
Jerry Andrew: 157
Jerry Leroy: 157
Randall Garrett: 157

Miller -
Susie Diane: 156

Mills -
Shirley 'Sandy': 142

Mitchell -
June Elaine: 140

Moceri -
David: 143
Jeffery Nicholas: 143
Kelsey: 143
Michael: 143
Michael John: 143
Michael Linn: 143
Monica Rosa: 143
Nicholas: 143
Terry: 143
Timothy: 143

Montgomery -
F.: 164

Moody -
Caleb E.: 151
Don: 151
Rev. Dwight Eugene: 151
Hannah M.: 151
Karis: 146
Olivia R.: 151
Ronnie Lee: 151

Moore -
Alvin Hooper: 145
Anna Frances: 146
Bessie Arlene: 146
Betty Susan 'Sue': 147
Brandon Joseph 'Jody': 155
Jacob: 147
Jimmy Donald: 145
Johnny Harold: 155
Jonathon Tyler: 155
Lydia: 147
Melody: 146
Micailah: 147
Ora Blanche: 146
Sandra Marlene: 145
Rev. Timothy Ray: 147
'Vance' Ray: 146

Morgan -
Gennie M.: 159

Moutos -
Deana: 148

N

Nation -
Chuck: 144
Flora Charleen Walker: 143
Jim: 144
Peggy Diane Walker: 143, 144
Sharon Yvonne Walker: 144

Nelson -
Dave: 142

Nix -
Wendy: 144

Norman -
Crystal Ann: 147
Lemuel: 147

Tammy Sue: 147

O
Orr -
Alina Marie: 160
Cecil Paul: 160

P
Paige -
Jeanette Elaine: 141
Parker -
Allison McKenzie: 155
Bertie Mae: 155
Blanche Arleen: 156
Christy Faye: 155
Clifford Dean 'Deano' , Jr.: 155
Rev. Clifford Dean , Sr.: 155
Jeff: 148
Lauren Elexis: 155
Mary Sue: 155
Misty Dawn: 155
Olean: 154
Otha Shelton: 160
Ronny: 148
Sarah Alice: 139
Steve 'Beav': 148
William Harry: 154
Payne -
Terry: 159
Petersen -
Kody Connor: 159
Kyle Christman: 159
Timothy Christman: 159
Phillips -
Andrew Peter: 168
Anna Laura: 150
Cynthia: 150
Daniel: 165
Eleanor "Nellie": 163
Horatio 'Rashio': 150
Jimmy: 150
Joan: 150
Kim: 150
Larry Dale: 150
Richard: 150

Plemmons -
Amy Michelle: 145
David Jenning: 146
Hannah Elizabeth: 146
Jeffrey: 146
Jennings Yates: 146
Kenneth Douglas: 146
Megan Nicole: 146
Stephen Jennings: 146
Tanner Ryan: 146
Tony Alvin: 146
William Andrew: 146
William Erick: 145
William Jenning: 145
William Michael: 145
Presley -
Carolyn: 150
Carroll Johnson: 150
Deborah: 150
Pressnell -
?: 159
Pyatte -
Brandon: 142
Damon: 142
Earl Detroy: 142
Harold Detroy: 142, 143
Jack Earl: 142
Jackie Rae: 142
Matthew: 142
Pauline April: 142
Rick Bruce: 142
Stacey Amber: 142
Tonya Rae: 142

Q
Queen -
Brian Jason: 139
Caryn Maria: 140
David Ronald: 140
Doris: 139
Johnnie 'Huff': 139
Lois: 159
Matthew David: 140
Nina Mae: 139
W. L.: 139

R

Raines -
Alice Jo: 142
Ralston -
Earl: 144
Moriah Yvonne: 144
Ratenski -
David: 153
Sean Michael: 154
Shawn Ian: 153
Raught -
Dale: 143
Ray -
Shelba Jean: 158
Renegar -
Sara Beth: 156
Rhodarmer -
Anita: 151
Ben: 151
Daughter: 151
First girl: 151
Fourth girl: 151
Kelly: 151
Second girl: 151
Third girl: 151
Thomas: 151
Rhodes -
Child: 158
Child: 158
Child: 158
Judy: 158
Woodfin: 158
Rogers -
Alan Dale: 150
Alvin: 150
Linda: 150
Patsey: 150
Rebecca: 150
Roles -
Wendy Beth: 146
Ross -
Elizabeth: 146
Roweder -
Linda: 147
Rowell -
Bruce: 143

Rebecca Dian: 144
Regan Renee: 144
Rick Mitchell: 143
Robert Dean: 144
Ryan Dean: 144
Ruler -
Amy: 143
Dave: 143
David: 143

S

Sam -
Deidre: 142
Sanders -
Megan Nicole: 156
William Frederick: 156
Scott -
Joseph: 141
Joseph Raymond: 141
Mishaela: 141
Nicole: 141
Seay -
Elizabeth Diane: 155
Self -
Billy: 149
Bryan: 149
Sharrmann -
Elizabeth: 167
Shilts -
Jackie: 152
Shook -
Christopher: 155
Shular -
Ora Blanche: 158
Sitton -
Brandy Marie: 152
Claude A.: 152
Daniel Ray: 152
David Allen: 152
David Allen: 152
Domenic Michael Austin: 152
Douglas Claude: 152
Ethel May: 153
Gertie: 153
Hazel: 147
Jeremy Loren: 152

Kathy Lee: 152
Kenneth Lee: 152
Shiann Marie: 152
Terry Allen: 152
Skelton -
Blaisha Leeann: 160
Holly Christine: 160
John Lee: 159
Kayla Justin: 160
Skipper -
Mary: 153
Slater -
Christine: 151
Sluder -
Michael Stuart: 157
Smathers -
Mary: 150
Smith -
Joshua Dale: 154
Raymond Ray: 154
Tiffany Olean: 154
Snider -
Bobbi Jean: 140
Bryan Matthew: 140
Carole Jean: 140
Cheryl: 140
Hunter Matthew: 140
Karen: 140
Michael: 140
Orray: 140
Steve: 140
Vernon Dean: 140
Snyder -
Wilsie/Elsie: 151
Sollid -
Marilyn: 147
Southards -
Gabriel: 155
Stamey -
Tracey Cheryl: 158
Standler -
Belinda: 149
Stephens -
Todd: 155
Stewart -
Dana Claire: 154

Swarner -
Pat: 140

T

Tackett -
Lon: 143
Lonzo Lee: 143
Luke Martin: 143
Talgenhoff -
Gail: 139
Taylor -
Cheyenne: 144
Dylan: 144
Jacob: 144
Jesse Bryson: 144
John Randall "Jody": 144
Kaityln: 144
Kody: 144
Randy: 144
William "Billy": 144
Thames -
Doug: 139
Dusty: 139
Gwen: 139
Nancy: 139
Rusty: 139
Susan: 139
Thompson -
Eric Wayne: 156
Gina Helen: 156
Joseph Paul: 156
Thornton -
Pearl: 139
Tieman -
Marlys: 147
Tishiyama -
Brenda: 149
Trantham -
Debra Lynn: 146
Glen Dexter: 146
Inavee: 148
Sandra Arlene: 146
Tuttle -
Caleb: 149
Jada Lea: 149
Joshua Silas: 150

Preston Stone: 149
Richie Dale: 150
Scott James: 149

V

Van Pelt -
Dylan James: 159
Ronnie Dean: 159
Vickers -
Barry Dwayne: 157
James Garland: 157
Katie Marie: 157
Melinda Hope: 157
Stephanie Lynna: 157
Vinson -
Rhonda: 149

W

Wakefield -
Denise: 143
Waldrop -
Susan: 154
Walker -
Arnold Lee: 143
Charley: 143
Jenny: 143
Keith: 143
Lisa: 143
Marty: 143
Ward -
Dwayne Calvin: 157
Joshua Calvin: 157
Tamayra Lynn: 157
Watson -
Alfred Lee: 157
Connie 'Michelle': 157
Ellen: 158
Janelle: 155
Travis Dale: 157
Wattenburger -
Daniel Curtis: 145
Mark: 145
Sarah Lynn: 145
Webb -
David: 141

Troy Raymond: 141
Tyler Charles: 141
West -
Jackie Lee: 157
Jessica Nicole: 157
Westfall -
Lisa: 156
Wheatley -
Gala Sue: 154
White -
Patti: 140
Wike -
Cheryle: 146
Williams -
Elsie Marie: 141
Sandy: 141
Williamson -
Parker Howell: 155
Travis Scott: 155
Willie Junior: 155
Willis -
Aleha Nicole: 149
Bradley: 149
Bryan Jeffrey: 149
Bryan Todd: 149
Rev. Calvin Clifford: 149
Gregory Preston: 149
James Lee: 149
Mathew Jason: 149
Megan: 149
Sherri Kay: 149
Wilson -
Laverne: 146
LaWonna: 141
Wiseman -
April Blaine: 159
Bob: 159
Wood -
Arta "Arty" Marie: 161
Henry: 163
James Bryson: 163
James? George?: 166
John: 166
Woodall -
Curtis: 147
Slater: 147
Tristan Montana: 147

Woolard -
    Matthew: 147
    Tucker Wesley: 147

Z
Zehnder -
    Gregory Scott: 144
    Jeffrey Alan: 144
    Kylee Anne: 144
    Leslie: 144
    Leslie Joseph: 144
    Sharie Lynn: 144